Surviving and Thriving:

Grief Relief & Continuing Relationships

Spirituality
WORKSHOPS

Jane V. Bissler, Ph.D., LPCC, FT

Deneene Florino

Sara Ruble

Cover design by Jon Kapper

Manufactured in the United States of America
10 9 8 7 6 5 4 3 2 1

For more copies call 330-221-4784
Website: www.spiritualityworkshops.com

Library of Congress Cataloging-in-Publication Data
Bissler, Jane V.
Florino, Deneene
Ruble, Sara
        Surviving and Thriving: Grief Relief &
        Continuing Relationships by Jane V. Bissler,
    Deneene Florino, Sara Ruble
        1. Surviving and Thriving: Grief Relief &
        Continuing Relationships

        ISBN-13: 978-0-9815979-0-4
        ISBN-10: 0-9815979-0-4

        2008

Table of Contents

Dedication

Deneene, Sara, and Jane wish to dedicate this book to Spirit. Without our knowledge, trust, and never-ending faith, we would not have had the foresight and energy to help those who are grieving. We praise Spirit for the inspiration we have felt and continue to lean into to bring this healing love to you.

We also dedicate this book to all those who have gone home before us. They, like you, are our true teachers. We continue to be open and to learn all that the universe has to offer and, to that, we are also dedicated.

Preface

"My wonderful son, Scott, has died. I can't imagine that he is gone forever and I will never see him, hear his voice, or feel his presence again. I can't live my life like this. Please help me!" These words are spoken all too often. As grieving people we want to know how to keep our loved ones in our lives. We want to know it is possible. We want to hear comforting words to assure us that the connections we had with our loved ones will continue. We call these "loving connections."

A field of research has developed from the need to continue this relationship. It is clinically called "continuing bonds." This research studies the impact of grief on those who believe their loved one is with them in some way. This can be as simple as trusting in the warmth of long-ago happenings, creating cherished memories, or as unique and compelling as knowing you hear your loved one in your everyday, present life.

This book is about the continuum of eternal bonds. Reading and applying the information will help you discern where you are on this scale and where you would like to be. It will help you explore your feelings about the difficult issues of grief. You will have the opportunity to understand how spirituality can be of great benefit to you, lessen your pain during the dark days of grief and form a connection with your loved one. Techniques creating this communication and awareness of how your spiritual beliefs can make your life more bearable and purposeful will be shown to you.

Sara's Story

On May 20, 1994, my life as I knew it changed forever. *Forever.* I came home from work and was gently told by my husband of nine months that my son, Scott, had died. Scott was nineteen years old. He was my only child and the love of my life. He was a healthy, bright, energetic college student who had gone to Colorado to work in a national park for the summer. He arrived at the park on Sunday and died of natural causes on Friday. This devastating news consumed me. The agony of Scott's life being over tore through me, and I was totally unprepared for a death of such unimaginable magnitude. I truly felt that my life had no meaning without Scott. There was no future I was interested in without him.

Looking back now, all these years later, even with the enormity of my grief and the pain that filled my soul, I clearly remember that there were many beautiful moments that encouraged me to go on. The most amazing of all was that I still had a connection with Scott. Whether it came through dreams, signs, or finding things, I KNEW Scott was still a part of my life. I had no idea things like that could happen! So, fortunately for me, Jane, who is my bereavement counselor, gave me the opportunity to share these seemingly wild and crazy things that were happening. She also gave me the validation and encouragement I needed to BELIEVE that those on the Other Side can and will let us know they are still around us. What sweet words for my broken heart. I began to read about such occurrences and the more I read and searched, the more my mind and heart were opened to a much bigger picture of life and death than I ever could have imagined existed. That was *very* comforting and it gave me a glimmer of hope that I desperately needed.

Even so, there remained much grief work for me to do, and whatever energy I had was directed to the many difficult issues that engulfed me. In time, I think I can say that I "fought the good fight" of grief until I couldn't fight it any longer. I was drained and depleted of energy. This is when I started to take a serious look at spirituality and, unquestionably, it breathed new life into me. I found, in spirituality, a belief system that didn't deny Scott was still very much a part of my life. It gave me hope for the future, and showed me that my life and my soul's journey are very, very important. I no longer feel like a victim; instead, I feel empowered. I am a *survivor*. This is not a journey without work, effort, and emotional investment, but I am extremely grateful for the answers and understanding I have gained by living a spiritual life. I now look forward to what the future holds for me. I hope by sharing my experiences you will gain insights to your grief and new hope for your future.

Deneene's Story

I was fortunate to be born into a family that nurtured my spirituality. My family did this both knowingly and not so knowingly. You see, my Aunt Lill (this is the "not so knowingly" part) had an altar of saints where she did novenas daily. When I was about 6 years old, I crept into her dark bedroom, lit only by the glowing candles on the altar, to hear my Aunt say her prayers aloud. It was surreal and eerie, and I loved the feeling. Each time I came into the room, Aunt Lill waved me over to kneel with her. She pointed to the saints and said, "See, they are smiling. It's going to be a good day." I wanted so much to see the saints smiling, but all I could see were 10 statues looking up at me.

One day while Aunt Lill and I were praying, she started to cry and say my cousin's name over and over again. My cousin was stationed overseas in the navy at that time. Aunt Lill told me to look at the saints so I could see that they were crying too. I tried very hard to see tears on the cheeks of the saints. I turned my head away in case they were embarrassed to cry in front of me, then quickly turned my head back around to catch them. Nothing. . . So, I closed my eyes and opened them really fast. I squinted. Again, nothing. . . I desperately wanted to see what my Aunt saw. Those saints were gateways to a mysterious world that I wished to observe and understand more than anything. Soon the phone rang. It was a naval officer saying that my cousin had been crushed by a piece of equipment and rushed to a hospital. We later found out that he would survive. Miraculously, he was able to recover from the injuries with only some minor back problems remaining.

Aunt Lill is a special lady with a gift that the family always talks about in hushes. My uncle would joke and ask her what pony to bet on when he was going to the track, and how the family would laugh. She never got the ponies right. After the day that my cousin was injured, I was brave enough to go alone into Aunt Lill's sanctuary with the altar of saints. I stared at the statues, closed my eyes, and even fell asleep in the altar's glow. I had become comfortable there because I knew it was a revered and holy place. It seemed like we had a secret in our house, and we were blessed to have a direct line of communication with God. One day when Aunt Lill was already at the altar, I sat down beside her wondering if it was going to be a good day or if another tragedy was going to happen to our family. As I sat there cross-legged, I closed my eyes and took a deep breath. I could feel the saints looking at me. I could feel them smiling. That's when I realized it was how the saints made her *feel* that my Aunt was trying to convey, not how they looked. At that remarkable moment, I began to learn about my own intuition and spirituality.

My Catholic upbringing in a devout Sicilian family taught me the fundamentals of the church's rituals. I went to catechism and made my communion. However, I never felt spirituality under the roof of the cathedral, but only at Aunt Lill's altar. My neighborhood also played a part in my spiritual growth. We lived in a northern Jewish suburb named Skokie in the Chicagoland area and were the only non-Jewish family for miles. When I was around 10 years old, my mom (this is the "knowingly" part) sent me to Hebrew school with my friends to show me the importance of learning how others believe and worship. The Hebrew school officials allowed me to stay in the temple, but did not let me go into the classes with my friends. Thus, I spent hours there listening to the cantor sing, reading in the library to learn about Hebrew philosophy, and waiting eagerly for Friday to arrive because I loved celebrating the Sabbath. I was drawn to the rituals of the Jewish religion as well. Even though I did not understand the Hebrew language, I could *feel* the presence of God as I attended the services. I have always enjoyed praying in groups because of this experience.

When I was about 12 years old, my dad (being the baby boomer that he is) decided he wanted to try Transcendental Meditation. So, he and I went to Evanston to find out about Maharishi Yogi, the famous guru who introduced the technique and also taught the Beatles to meditate. We visited one of the Maharishi's temples. I thought it was the coolest thing—candles, incense, people levitating—unbelievable. Of course, I wanted to learn all about it. The instructors took me into a room alone, gave me my very own secret mantra, and proceeded to teach me about breathing and relaxation. Then, Dad and I watched tapes of the Maharishi speaking about enlightenment and peace. I was in my glory. Nothing at school or in the outside world intrigued me more than all of these spiritual experiences.

My mom's adult best friend, Judy, was her childhood friend from grammar school. Judy's two children, Cyndie and David, and I were born just years apart and spent all of our time together. I loved them so much that they were like a sister and brother to me, and Judy was like a second mom. When Cyndie was 19 and I was 17, Cyndie committed suicide. I was the one who found her. This tragic event changed my life profoundly. Not only did I have to deal with the life-changing trauma of Cyndie's death, but also the loss of my beloved best friend and her family. None of us were ever the same after that horrific day and emotions ran high. We all drifted in our own sorrow.

Because I was the one who found Cyndie after her death, my family went into "Sicilian crisis drama mode." Of course, being as religious as they all were, they recounted the Catholic beliefs on suicide which meant Cyndie went to hell or, if by some chance she talked her way out of that (she *was* good at talking), for sure was sent to purgatory to wander through eternity with the other unfortunate souls. I actually had to be rebaptized, and entire congregations to which my family members and their friends belonged held masses and services for me. In their eyes, I had rubbed elbows with the devil and everyone was in high alert to save my soul. I just could not fathom such thoughts. How could someone I knew and loved on such a deep level go to hell? It was at this sagacious moment that my belief system started to take a shape of its own. I wanted answers to my questions about heaven and hell from an unbiased party. I wanted to know death.

Okay, at this point, I need to backtrack a little. In September of the previous year, right before my 16th birthday, my grandfather died of stomach cancer. He was not on hospice. Grandfather passed away in a hospital room writhing in pain, and we as a family stood by helpless with tears in our eyes as we listened to him scream in agony. I knew there had to be a better way. And, crouched at the back of his room, I silently promised him that I would find it. Grandfather's death was the first loss of a loved one that I had experienced and my grief was more painful than I ever could have imagined. I cried for Grandfather, for me, and for my father.

Almost a year to the day after Grandfather's death, this time just days after my birthday, Cyndie died. Wow. . . I was still reeling from Grandfather's death. Luckily enough, my Aunt Phil's house became my refuge. I would go there to feel safe and loved. Aunt Phil and her family were night owls and, in the darkest part of the night when I could not sleep, I found myself getting into my car and soon there I would be, turning the knob of her door that was always open. I'd come in with tearstained cheeks at 2 or 3 a.m. and my aunt would greet me, hug me, tell me there was food on the stove, and act as if it was noontime on Sunday. We'd watch old movies together until I'd fall asleep on the couch. At sunrise, I'd awaken still feeling in a fog from the night before. Yet, I found peace there. I found quiet. Even if only for a few hours, my head and my heart were able to shut off the never-ending noise, the grief streaming from inside. Here, in one of the busiest homes I knew between midnight and 6 a.m., I was able to find serenity and safety.

Well, the following spring, my Aunt Phil died of a heart attack. No way, not again, not another loss! I could not bear it. I could not go to her funeral I had no heart left to break. I had nowhere to go. Consequently, I began a journey within myself. I met a wonderful tutor who helped me study for my SATs. Phyllis was more than a tutor. She was a life coach; well, at least for me. She would stop whatever we were doing, take off her glasses, and listen to me for hours. Phyllis helped me regain my self-esteem and find my way back at the very lowest point in my life. She showed me that I had the courage to go on despite my grief and enter college. My life changed remarkably after I walked into Phyllis's office. To this day, she is one of my dearest friends.

One of the things that took me a long time to comprehend after Cyndie died was the finality of her being gone. I could not pick up the phone and call her. She was nowhere to be found. And, I did try to find her. I caught myself looking everywhere for her because I was not completely convinced that death meant "gone." I finally came up with the delusion that Cyndie's death was all a big plot for her to start life anew. This fantasy allowed me to believe that she had staged her death. The real Cyndie had actually been whisked off in a jet to another part of the world to begin an exciting romantic adventure. I was convinced that someday, when she thought it was safe and no one was looking, Cyndie would return to the States and I'd just happen to be there to rejoice in our long-awaited reunion. This dream made the loss a little more tolerable. To think of her somewhere else on this earth enabled me to get through my days and, more importantly, my nights. For many years, I looked for Cyndie, my search unconsciously programmed in the scanning of any crowd. And, 25 years later, I still catch myself looking.

Thus, as part of the journey within me, I had to discover what death was all about. I majored in theology at college so I could learn about the ways that the faithful in all religions view life and perceive death. I encountered another most amazing teacher, Dr. Wendell Beane, and he gifted me with the permission to break free from the chains of Catholicism and to embrace what resonated within my soul. I studied about a fascinating psychiatrist, Elisabeth Kübler Ross, and, while reading her classic work *On Death and*

Dying in the library on a rainy Monday afternoon, I vowed to meet her. I knew she would help me understand how to comfort the dying so that the promise I made to my grandfather would be kept.

I was then 20 years old and, in my 30th year, I did meet Elisabeth Kübler Ross and we became friends. It was right before she had her first stroke and I was fortunate enough to help care for her after she became ill. I went to her home after work and we'd eat popcorn, watch *Star Trek*, and philosophize about life, death, and the afterlife. By that time, I had become a hospice spiritual care and bereavement counselor and Elisabeth always wanted to read the memorials I was writing. With her thick accent, she'd give me her "two cents," which I was more than honored to receive.

As you can see, I came to know death so that it was no longer a stranger to me. Hospice taught me all about pain control and how to work as a team to accord patients the dignity they deserve in their final days. I was immersed in patients' philosophies, their life stories, and how each viewed life and death. I comforted patients and their families while these men and women lifted the veil from this world to the next. It was a privilege to be there, in the presence of the Divine.

By the time I'd worked 10 years in hospice, I had counseled over 10,000 patients and family members during the dying or bereavement process. I often was a witness to what some would call "unexplainable events," or "miracles." I have sincerely come to believe that the loved ones who have died before us, along with our other angels, will come to take our hands and guide us to the next world. We will move slowly from one realm of existence to another, all along the way becoming comfortable in our new surroundings, seeing old familiar faces and places, and being able to let go of life here on Earth. This will allow us to release the loved ones left behind, now confident that we will see them again, never be far from them, and remain in their lives forever.

Death has a profound effect on the living. We need death and loss in order to put earthly life in perspective. Death and loss are catalysts for spiritual growth. It is in the times of deepest despair that we reach out to God and surrender. Through this surrender, we find ourselves and our connectedness. We achieve the understanding that we are not far apart from anything; that we are everything; that within us are the key, the road map, and the encoding to existence and to all.

I would like to take this moment in time to thank the other very important people that whom without I would never had made it to be where I am today. This would include: my mother, father, siblings, extended family, and friends. You all know who you are and for you I am eternally grateful.

Jane's Story

I began working with grieving people while helping my husband with his funeral business. He asked me to start a program where the families that he lovingly cared for during the funeral process could be helped after the burial. I developed a program to contact all of the families who said they wanted to be contacted six weeks after the funeral. I visited with these people, and soon realized that most of the families who really needed help where those whose adolescent children had died suddenly. In fact, many bereaved parents began scheduling appointment times with me even if they hadn't used my husband's funeral home.

I learned that those of us in the counseling profession didn't know how to help this population. I did some research to see what, from a bereaved parent's perspective, was most helpful. The primary result of this study was that these parents wished to have a continuing relationship with their child. I began to listen for ways that they were seeking meaning from their loss. They talked about the memories they had with their child, and these were more bitter than sweet. A few of my clients spoke of ways that they still felt connected to their child. And, fewer still, spoke about ways they were connecting in new ways with their loved one.

Around this time, I was able to attend a workshop presented by Bill and Judy Guggenheim, the authors of *Hello From Heaven* (New York: Bantam, 1996). The Guggenheims studied several thousand people who had after-death communications. The stories that these authors reported sounded very similar to the ones that my clients were sharing. This opened up a new area of study for me, not only through books and research, but through personal experience.

My dad was a gruff, World War II veteran. He had a heart of gold and I found out in the autumn years of his life, Dad was the world's biggest softie.

For several years, he suffered with congestive heart failure and became a shell of the man he once had been. The disease changed his personality and though our relationship had been based on mutual respect and a genuine love for each other, his new softness had presented opportunities for open conversation.

During the last several months of his illness, I was fortunate to be able to spend several afternoons each week with him. My mother was his care-taker and I was able to visit without needing to shoulder much of the everyday responsibility.

I began to privately talk with my father about his death. At times, he would be willing to discuss the eventuality. But most of the time, he would talk about going to the Cleveland Clinic and asking for a heart transplant. Even at the age of 82, he wasn't ready to give up and return "home" without a fight.

During one visit, I was sitting beside his bed when he began speaking from a soul level. It's hard to describe what that is, but if attuned to the subtle nuisances of voice and subject matter, you know it when you hear it. I knew my chance had come.

"Dad, I believe you can contact me from

heaven."

His crystal clear blue eyes snapped to attention and seemed to bore a hole into my brown ones.

"I don't know about such things, honey. Maybe you should tell me more."

"I know a lady who took care of her sister. They established a sign that when petals fell from flowers, it was her saying she had made it to heaven and all was well. I believe we can set up a sign you can give me."

"Hmmm, well let me think about that."

A calm and thoughtful quietness engulfed the room. Soon he spoke again.

"Well what would we do?"

"I don't know Dad, what are you thinking?" After some discussion, we decided to think and talk about it later. It was a reprieve, as I wasn't prepared to go further into the conversation.

The next several days were not good ones for Dad. He was sleeping most of the time and when awake, incoherent. I was afraid I had lost my opportunity and he would die before we could complete our plans. I felt I had missed an opening, but convinced myself that perhaps the seed had been planted and it would blossom into a loving connection.

A week later, he was talking and was mentally aware. I seized the chance to talk with him.

"Dad, do you remember our conversation of a few days ago?" Immediately he looked at me and was again fully alert.

"I'll bet we have the same idea for a sign and we could say it together", he answered. "Ready?"

I was surprised because I had not considered what the sign might be.

"Ok, I'll count to three. One, two, three", Dad said.

"Rainbows," we said, in unison.

He seemed very satisfied and drifted off to sleep. It would be the last "good" day he would have. He died three days later.

I decided not to tell anyone of this discussion and resultant promise for fear it would not work and my mother would be heart-broken, again.

My husband and I have a motor home and we love to travel with our two daughters. The year my father died, my mother joined us on our annual trip. We decided to make our last stop Cook's Forest in Pennsylvania. It was one of my Dad's favorite spots and it was a tribute to him that we stopped there before returning home.

It was late in the afternoon when we arrived at our campsite. Clouds were rolling in - giving relief to the 90-degree heat. As I readied the picnic table for our evening meal, I felt a few sprinkles and hurried inside to wait for the rain to pass. When I came back outdoors, I heard my father's voice.

"Jane, look up."

Instantly, I followed his command and saw a

beautiful double rainbow. I called for everyone to come out. With tears running down my face, I explained to my family the plan that Dad and I had agreed on. I knew he was keeping his agreement.

My husband, Rick, let me know that today marked the one month anniversary of my father's death.

Within a day or two of his death date for fifteen months, I saw a rainbow. It didn't matter where I was - at home, in Argentina, in Chicago or flying on an airplane. As a result of this loving connection with my dad, I gained a confidence in my spiritual beliefs and a thirst for more information about the loving connections of others.

I had been told stories of predetermined connections in my professional life as a counselor. Having this personal experience created my interest in researching the topic even more. I also knew both from research and personal experience having a continuing relationship with a loved one was the most important aspect of assimilating the loss of my father into my life. The connections I experienced from my dad gave me the confidence I needed to share the personal reality of connections with my clients. In fact, my story became a format for the goals my clients set for their own loving connections.

Presently, I know that my clients who have after-death communications with their loved ones have a stronger will to live, more joy in their lives, and a better assimilation of the death. They also practice a personal spirituality that gives them a way to increase these communications and feel a sense of control over their lives.

Writing this book with Deneene and Sara is a way of spreading the news that living a spiritual life, through organized religion or on your own thoughts and beliefs, brings peace and tranquility to grieving people. The chapters have been set up to provide you with a needed foundation as well as practical and understandable ways to form this belief system and invite your loved one into your life in a new and loving way.

Introduction

Spiritual connections, sometimes called "continuing bonds," "loving connections," or "continuing relationships," provide a way for us to include a loved one who has died in our life through the creation of symbols, images, and signs that are both powerful and essential for their continuing survival. It is clear that the death of a loved one does not end a relationship. Whether or not this relationship is transformed to a spiritual one, our loved ones are not forgotten just because they are no longer in their physical bodies. We talk about them, miss them, and most of us even find ourselves talking to them. However, creating a spiritual connection with them involves taking the relationship on a new path, just as if they had reached a new developmental stage in life and we'd need to find a new way to connect with them. A spiritual or loving connection is a different kind of relationship, but one that at times is even stronger than the one we had with them when they were on Earth. Our spiritual connection doesn't die with our loved ones. How could it? Our energy is derived from God or, as some say from Spirit, and returns to God. Just because we'd no longer have a physical body, how could it be that we wouldn't continue to be a loved one? How could these connections not be Spirit given?

To continue an explanation of our loved one's transformation, think of it this way. Take an ice cube out of your freezer and put in on the sidewalk. After a time, you will see a little puddle of water and the ice cube is no longer there. Again, more time passes and what happens to the puddle? Can you see it any longer? Does it make sense to you to say that it has disappeared and it no longer exists? Most of us would say that the water was in solid form when it was ice, in liquid form when it was the puddle, and in gas form when it evaporated from the sidewalk. It may be a bit of a stretch to think of human life in this way, but it may help to know that the water from the ice cube is still as real as your loved one is. It just is in another form.

For healthy after-death connections, the relationship with our loved one must be reorganized and the loss assimilated in a way so that there is an openness for the communications to be heard, felt, and sometimes even seen. When this is accomplished, we will find hopefulness and be able to make a commitment to have our loved one be a part of our present and future without losing the past. Whatever connection is made—whether through a sign, symbol, thought, dream, or doing an act in the loved one's name—it is this loving connection that seems to help us look toward the future and be willing to enter into life again.

This book has three goals in mind. First, we want to help you explore your own belief structure.

We will do this by presenting a historical and contemporary synopsis of major religions and belief structures. We will also present questions for you to ponder and, hopefully, actually answer in the privacy of your own home.

Our second goal is for you to use the information presented here to form the foundation for living a more spiritual life. By formulating your plan and enacting it one manageable bite-sized piece at a time, we hope that you will be able to attain the joy felt by others we have had the pleasure of working with. Therefore, the third goal is to create an continuing relationships with your loved ones in spirit. Nothing is more important to your future happiness and ability to do the work of living this human existence.

Our personal and professional experiences have led us to write this book and share these teachings with you. Because we have seen and experienced the joy that living this type of life brings, we feel compelled to share this information and wisdom with you. We wish you many wonderful loving connections.

Understanding Personal Spiritual Beliefs and How We Use Them

Knowing our own spiritual beliefs, standards, and ethics adds significant value to life. This value increases our joy, and allows us to cherish our own life and those of our loved ones, both alive and deceased. Spirituality sets the stage for transcendence in life. It organizes our experiences by creating more awareness and appreciation of the different dimensions to life beyond self. It allows us to create a relationship with an increased awareness of a connection with ourselves, others, God/Spirit/Divinity, and nature. Becoming spiritually aware is an unfolding of life that calls for reflection and experience, including a sense of who we are and how we know what we know.

Individual people have different theories about where the soul goes after death. There even are those who believe in no afterlife; that is, when we die, we die and there is no consciousness. Sometimes, during the course of a lifetime, people's ideas and opinions about life after death change. And, there are many who are not yet sure of what they believe and are searching for answers. Deneene, Jane, and Sara believe that all theories and opinions are good if they feel right and resonate with the individual. We respect all of you for where you are, and we are not trying to talk you into or out of what you believe. We ourselves believe in reincarnation and the belief of karma and, although our opinions may be different from some of you, the content of these pages will certainly still be of much value.

Before beginning this book, it's important to know what your own beliefs are. We would like you to take a few moments now to answer the questions listed below. In doing so, you will learn what your beliefs are in regard to connecting with yourself, your loved ones, and others. You will be asked to answer these questions again at the end of the book, and seeing how different your answers are then will be important to your future development. Please choose a special place to write down your answers, perhaps in a journal to keep on a night table so that you can record your dreams and thoughts as you go through this life-changing process. Be as specific as you can be because knowing every nuance of your thoughts today will further your work and ultimate connections later.

1. What is your definition of spirituality and continuing relationships?
2. If you woke up tomorrow morning and you were the spiritual person that you wanted to be, what would you be doing differently?
3. How do you think a new spirituality and loving connections will help you?
4. How do you think your spirituality and these connections have helped you in the past?
5. What questions do you have about spirituality and making these connections?
6. How would living a more spiritual life affect your afflictions: fear, anger, regret, guilt?
7. How will your grief be affected by living a spiritual life?
8. What in your life has brought you to your present spiritual beliefs?

GRIEF RELIEF

1

Spirituality and Religion:
Is There a Difference?

Do we need to care about this issue? How will it affect our spirituality, our personal growth, and our loving connections? We believe that knowing our feelings about spirituality and religion can be a powerful tool in living a more spiritual life. Many of us were raised in organized religious communities. It may be difficult for us to feel that we are moving away from our upbringing and, at times, this can cause us to feel guilty. This chapter is designed to help you ascertain your feelings, and possibly develop your knowledge about spirituality. It is our hope that you will find a harmonic balance between your spirituality and your religious beliefs.

We will present both historical and contemporary perspectives of spiritual beliefs within several organized religions. Lastly, we will present possible roadblocks to gaining a more spiritual belief structure. We'll begin by sharing with you our viewpoint about spirituality *in* religion and spirituality *as opposed to* religion.

In recent years, *spirituality in religion* has carried connotations of a believer having a faith that is more personal, less dogmatic, and more open to new ideas and influences. It is also rich in a more pluralistic belief structure than the dogmatic faiths of mature religions. This kind of spirituality can bring to the forefront the nature of the believer's personal relationship or "connection" with their Higher Power. Being spiritual within an organized religion usually means that the person has a greater personal relationship with their God, Spirit, or Higher Power. At times, this separates them from some of the members of their organized faith.

Those who speak of *spirituality as opposed to religion* generally believe there are many spiritual paths. They deny there is any one objective truth about the best path to follow. Rather, adherents of this definition of the term emphasize the importance of finding one's own path to God, Spirit, or their Higher Power. An individual's decision is made about what road to take instead of just following what others say. In short, the path that makes the most coherent sense becomes the correct one to be followed.

Historical Perspective

The spiritual underpinnings of the major religions are beautiful and poignant. In sharing a few brief comments about several of these beliefs, we hope this information will provide a foundation for your individual spiritual beliefs.

Islam

Muslims believe that one personal God

Almighty exists. Their creator is all powerful and is formless, meaning that the God they believe in has never taken human form. God is the only one worshipped. Muhammad is revered as the greatest and final prophet. Jesus Christ is seen as a prophet who performed miracles and will return as a Muslim. However, they do not believe Jesus was an incarnation of God.

Muslims also believe that their deceased loved ones will experience all that heaven has to offer and that unsaved souls will experience the torture of hell. God will resurrect the dead, uniting the body and soul, and will make the decision for the deceased to go to one of seven layers of heaven or to hell. People have the ability to choose right or wrong and what they believe. This faith also believes in Satan, but they feel that Satan has no power over the Muslim people.

Hinduism

Many Hindus believe in Brahman (God) as the ultimate soul. There are many gods and goddesses named in this faith. These are all representatives of the One Supreme God. Hinduism has a trinity of Brahman as the creator (Brahma), the preserver (Vishnu), and the destroyer (Shiva) of the universe. There are many, if not countless, incarnations and manifestations of God.

Hinduism works through the laws of karma. A person may be reborn into a number of heavens and hells, depending on the karma earned during their lifetime. Hindus believe that the soul is reborn until it reaches the enlightenment phase and then is liberated from rebirth. The illusion of evil is extinguished through enlightenment. After this is earned, the soul enters a state of ultimate bliss.

Buddhism

Mahayana Buddhists

This type of Buddhism includes diverse beliefs and trends. The main sects are Pure Land, Zen, and Vajravana Buddhism. There is no Creator or ruler God in this belief system. There is, however, a belief in The Three Bodies or forms of Buddha. The first is the Body of Essence; the second, the Body of Bliss; and the third, the Body of Transformation. Enlightenment is achieved by becoming one with the Ultimate Reality and experiencing Infinite Bliss.

Karma is a big part of the belief structure of this faith. Buddhists believe that a person's wholesome or unwholesome intentions become imprinted in the mind and this creates what happens in the next life. Any negativity creates a persistence of negativity in rebirth. The goal of these lifetimes is enlightenment leading to Nirvana. This community of believers uses Four Noble Truths and an Eightfold Path to show the way to this ultimate joy. Of course, worshipping Buddha is the essential truth and task. What is sought is extinguishment of all worldly cravings, desires, and attachments through loving kindness, compassion, charity, moral conduct, wisdom, and meditation.

Theravada Buddhism

Buddha, "the Awakened One," is revered above all. Buddha is considered as the supreme sage and the absolute mode of a fully enlightened person. Buddha is believed to have been human and a fully enlightened spiritual teacher and inspiration. There is no God in this belief system, so Buddha is the one and only to be admired and revered.

Karma is followed in this belief community as well. One's goodness and decentness is what determines whether the soul continues to be reborn or reaches the end of the cycles of rebirth and enjoys Nirvana for eternity.

Taoism

Believers of Taoism search for the ultimate reality. The Supreme Being or ultimate truth is beyond words and is not generally referred to as God. There are also no incarnations of the supreme being and death has no particular meaning to Taoists.

Taoists believe in dualities. This means that all positions or emotions have their opposite. For example, Taoists believe that the opposite of good is evil. These words and the actions associated with them have opposite words and actions as well. They also believe that when one emotion is expressed (for example, good), it automatically creates the opposite, which is evil. These emotions are two actions at opposite ends of the same spectrum, and each action has some of the other included in it. The Taoists make a distinction between considering the reality of good and evil instead of focusing on the concept of good and evil. Knowing and attending to the differences between reality and concept is a main tenet of this belief system.

Judaism

Reformed Jewish Beliefs

This sect believes that there is one God Almighty who is all powerful and all knowing. Their God is also formless. There are no incarnations of God, and Moses was the greatest of all prophets. God is also believed to control all phenomena.

Reformed Jews have no official position regarding the afterlife. Some believe in heaven and hell as a state of consciousness however, others believe in reincarnation and some may not believe in an afterlife at all. Although the major belief is that God is all forgiving, the main emphasis is on living the kind of life that God commands and this will assure one of salvation. Reformed Jews also believe that humans have free will and God joins the faithful in their suffering.

Orthodox Jewish Beliefs

Several belief structures are the same in the Reformed and Orthodox Jewish beliefs. Namely, there is one God Almighty who is all powerful and all knowing. Second, both believe that God is formless. Third, there are no incarnations of God, and Moses was the greatest of all prophets.

This traditional form of Judaism believes in the world to come, the coming of the Messiah, and a resurrection of the dead. However, some beliefs vary on the details. Some Orthodox Jews believe that the souls of the virtuous go to heaven, or are reincarnated, while the evil experience a hell of their own making or remain dead. Some believe God will bring back to life the honorable to live on Earth after the Messiah comes to purify the world. Judaism generally focuses on strictly following God's commandments rather than on details of the afterlife or rewards after death.

Christianity

Catholics

Catholics believe in the trinity of the Father (God), the Son (Christ), and the Holy Spirit. These entitles comprise the one God Almighty. They believe that Jesus Christ is God's one and only son. Catholics believe that God immediately judges who will go to heaven, purgatory, or hell. It is believed that if God sends a loved one to purgatory, the prayers of the survivors can move that person on to heaven. Otherwise, the person will be sent to hell. They believe that whether reward or punishment is received after death is commensurate to the life that they lived. Hell is seen as the pain that results when the person is separated from God. This faith believes that Christ will return at the end of the world and he will judge all humans.

Catholics also believe that Satan roams the earth which causes pain and suffering. God's design is to test, strengthen beliefs, and teach. The greater reward will be gained after death in heaven or hell.

Conservative Protestants

This faith views the Holy Bible as the final and only authority over all humans. Conservative Protestants believe in the Trinity of the Father (God), the Son (Christ), and the Holy Spirit that comprises one God Almighty. Jesus Christ is seen as God's only son. Souls experience heaven or hell depending on their behavior during life. Some, however, believe that souls will remain "asleep" until the resurrection and the final judgment day.

Conservative Protestants also believe in original sin, meaning that Adam and Eve caused all humans to have this sin. Many of this faith believe that only a few people will be saved and, to be among the few, one must have and express their complete faith in Jesus Christ as their one Lord and Savior. Speaking in tongues and preaching the gospel are often considered as evidence of being saved.

Liberal Protestants

This belief community views the Bible as the word of God. Liberal Protestants also believe in the Trinity of the Father (God), the Son (Christ), and the Holy Spirit that comprises one God Almighty. Jesus Christ is believed to be the Son of God. All believers are thought to be sons and daughters of God, and that Christ is perfect.

Liberal Protestants believe that goodness will somehow be rewarded and evil will be punished after death. They believe that Jesus died for their sins and if they ask for forgiveness, God forgives them.

Unitarian Universalists

This community of people welcome all beliefs. Some believe in incarnations and some believe in the embodiment of God. Some believe Christ is God's Son. Most Unitarian Universalists believe that the Bible is a symbolic book and that natural processes account for the origins of man. Heaven and hell are believed to be states of consciousness either in life or after death. Some believe in reincarnation and some believe there is nothing after death.

Most Unitarian Universalists do not believe in original sin or that Satan exists. If there is a belief in God, it is thought that God is good, and that God made people good and gave them free will. Many believe there is a separation from God when people are immoral. Others believe in karma and still others believe that wrongdoing is a matter of human nature.

New Age

God is the life force, awareness, ultimate truth. God is formless and alive within all people and matter. God is in all and all are of God. Most believe there are no incarnations of God because everyone in the universe is of God.

Some believe in a continual rebirth and others believe that their souls rest for a period of time before deciding on whether to accept a new body to come to Earth in. They also believe that heaven and hell are states of consciousness and are self-imposed. These negative states are due to an ignorance of God as being all.

Contemporary Spirituality

Global consciousness has evolved to the point that the option of "choice" about our religious beliefs—our spiritual consciousness—is now easier than ever before. With this comes the freedom to break from old ideologies, listen to the voice of our soul, and follow our intuition.

The roots of this transformation are seated in the 1960s when we as Americans began demanding freedom to choose the life we wanted to live, one that reflected who we were inside. The 1960s paved the way to open thinking, where we took heed of our own consciousness and acted on what it was telling us. We expressed ourselves in song, and sometimes even in drugs and sex. After decades of racial oppression, we finally became a nation in living color. Eastern religious thinking streamed across the borders, bringing enlightenment to mingle with the Christian doctrines of the West.

Today's generation has been born into this new thinking. We don't think twice about scheduling retreats, something our parents thought only priests and monks attended, for all types of spiritual modalities. We practice yoga as an exercise when, at one time, this powerful metaphysical tradition was practiced exclusively by devout Hindus in India. Displayed prominently in our living rooms are sacred texts that those who walked this earth before us coveted, gave their lives to write, and hid so that they would not be taken and destroyed. Because of the high-tech revolution and the Internet, holy manuscripts can be read online, printed out, and carried around by anyone. This ease of access to sacred writings has sometimes made us lose sight of their holiness.

In previous decades, others would have laughed at anyone who told them that they wanted to follow their inner calling and act on their intuition. But, nowadays, people don't think twice about allowing us the space to explore our soul and search out our mission. Earlier generations were tightly closed about their religiosity and political beliefs, so much so that it was considered rude to ask someone about their views. Today, we proudly parade our beliefs on T-shirts and bumper stickers. Our parents had difficulty saying something like "my inner calling tells me I should be a writer, a healer, or an acupuncturist." Now, we can say freely, "I think I would like to try meditation, go on a Zen retreat, or study the Kabbalah." Our self-esteem soars as we pursue such endeavors.

Fear of disgrace used to imprison self-esteem in the dark. Families kept secrets about everything from unwed mothers to mental disorders to homosexuality. Thankfully, contemporary consensus is to talk openly about our struggles in public. There even are Internet chat rooms about how to cope with just about everything. Common sense has streamed into our psyche to expose our deepest, darkest fears and help us get over their shame. In years past, those who were intuitively psychic also were ridiculed and the objects of gossip. Sometimes these people even were killed because of their psychic powers or ability to communicate with the deceased. Now, psychics have their own TV shows and tour the country promoting their bestsellers. Their ability to talk to the Other Side is revered by those who believe in their power. Law enforcement even takes advantage of the talents of psychics to find missing people and solve cases. Many are openly trying to nurture that part of their selves and there are workshops, meditation groups, relaxation groups, and soul companions with whom this need can be nurtured

Mainstream religion is also perceived differently now. Of course, there still are people who repeat their prayers, confess, and expect to be saved because they sit in a church pew every Sunday. This is not the meaning of being one of God's people. However, there are others who want to understand the metaphysics behind their religion. They want to read and study the Gnostic gospels, the Koran, and the Kabbalah to learn that all the sacred texts were originally written to impart the same meaning. The purpose of these writings was not to start religious wars or to control the masses, but to spread unconditional love and an understanding of humankind's higher purpose here on Earth. Through our belief in what feels right, we are able to question, discover, and decide for ourselves the path that our individual spirituality will take. We can then take over the controls of our life to achieve what we are meant to do on this planet and fulfill our true purpose.

Spirituality and Religion from the Perspective of a Grieving Mother, Sara

In grief and loss, our faith is often shattered. . . . we are lost and broken and desperately searching for help. Our belief system is suddenly thrown totally off balance. As a bereaved mom, I had a million questions following Scott's sudden death that *no one* could answer to my satisfaction. Many of my questions were about God or what I had been taught about God and heaven through organized religion. I was angry, confused, and lost. I needed answers, *real* answers.

For me, questions or issues about a Higher Power or God, as I will refer to this entity, arose immediately. I had mostly connected God with organized religion. That's how I knew God. Before I could even catch my breath and realize what had just happened . . . that Scott had suddenly *died*, we had to plan a funeral. A *funeral for my only child*. Those life-shattering words should never have been thought of, whispered, or uttered. Somehow, without our consent, life and society pushed us and we had to undertake this arduous task. We had to plan Scott's funeral. We were immediately faced with choosing just the right prayers, music, and biblical readings. They would be all about God and love and Scott being in a safe place. On that dark day of Scott's funeral, I hoped those carefully chosen words would help me, but they turned out to be just words. I needed something far greater than those "words" to help my broken heart. The beautiful music was momentarily soothing and I was grateful for that. What I found to be most comforting at Scott's funeral were the many people who came to remember him, and their kindness. I could feel their love.

Almost immediately after Scott died, I heard many comments that included "God." I knew these friends were looking for any words to help me. . . . I may have even used a few of these statements myself when I was trying to soothe others in their loss. Of course, this was before my Scott died. As I listened to "It was God's will," "God takes the young," or "God doesn't give us more than we can bear," my questions about God increased. *Could I believe any of those statements?* I needed to hang on to something, but I also really needed the *truth* about God, and life and death and what that was all about. Where could I find the truth?

Many, many more questions arose within me . . . seethed within me. Why did Scott die? Why would a loving God let this happen to Scott and to me? Did I do something wrong? Why was I being punished? Certainly Scott was not being punished, he was too good for that! Doesn't God protect us? Isn't that what I was taught in Sunday school? Should I still pray to God? How can he help me now? I desperately needed to KNOW that Scott was in heaven. I wanted to scream at those who were telling me he *is* in heaven. How do you *know* for sure? I had an overall anger and rage at God because he should NOT have let this happen to Scott. Aren't we taught in church how much God loves us? We try to be so good to prevent this kind of thing from happening.

I think though, deep down in my heart, I really did not want to believe God had anything to do with Scott's death. I wanted to believe in something . . . anything that would bring me comfort. There were so many questions and so few answers that made sense to me at that most difficult time.

I realize now that death or loss forces these questions in many of us.

As I spoke with others who had lost a loved one, I found that, even if they had a strong religious background prior to the death, they reacted in different ways. A few went more deeply into their faith without question. Their belief in God did not waiver. Others questioned what they had been taught by their church and were so mad at God, or their Higher Power, that they turned away from their religion. Others searched further by talking with their ministers, priests, rabbis, and other church leaders for answers to their tough questions. Often the answers were not helpful. I met many people who were very mad at God and I wondered if their faith had brought them any consolation. I also found that many, like me, did not know what direction to go in.

My organized religious background had been one of attending church as a child, first the

Lutheran Church and then the Episcopal Church that was built in our neighborhood. The Episcopal Church was convenient so it gave my brothers, my sister, and me the opportunity to participate in church-related activities. For our family though, it was not the dogma or the beliefs of a particular church that brought us there, it was more to be involved, to learn about God, and for me, to sing in the choir with my friends. It was social and we liked to go. I went to Sunday School, but did not get much out of the teachings and prayers. It all seemed so mechanical to me and also a lot of work in memorizing the prayers. It was more like, "Believe this . . . because we say you should." The actual meaning was lost on me. Later on, I attended another church after I married my first husband. He was Catholic and I attended church with him and participated, but never was able to connect with the religious teachings. We're all so different in our beliefs.

This obviously was not a strong background in organized religion, but I had always believed in a loving God and trusted that if I was good, God would take care of my family and me. Now, as I faced the reality of Scott's death, I was forced to look deeper as I searched for questions that seemed to have no answers. I was constantly examining God and religion because it seemed the answers should be there. Who else has anything to do with death?

The Bible, filled with scripture, helped

some grieving people who I knew. I was aware of the fact the Bible had been edited time and time again by vast numbers of people throughout thousands of years, sometimes adding their own perspective. I questioned its validity. I'd ask, "How can I be sure this is really God's word?"

Organized religions are man-made, often big businesses like televangelism, and I just didn't think I'd be able to believe everything they were teaching. I had not invested in that kind of religion before and continued to keep my distance.

I did believe in heaven. I HAD to. I stopped questioning this. Scott *had* to be safe in heaven and that was one thing that I hung on to. I would trust there was a heaven and that brought me some much-needed peace. I would picture him high above the clouds in a beautiful place with lush gardens playing soccer or doing whatever he wanted to. Even if I was in a state of devastation, it truly helped me to believe that Scott was happy and safe.

I questioned hell. I had trouble believing a loving God would send people to a place such as hell. Actually, I was *living my own hell* with Scott's death. That WAS hell! Pain and anguish overwhelmed me day in and day out. There was so much to endure, often too much to even comprehend.

I was confused and curious about God, about death, about the need for religion for me. I wondered if we were getting what we needed from religious teachings, especially in grief. Spirituality was kind of an unknown for me at that point, but I think many of the beliefs were there. I just had never given them a "name." I was certainly becoming open to new ideas, because the old ones were not working for me.

I continued to pray to, talk with, and beg God for help, hoping some miracle could rectify all this, or that perhaps it was time for me to die too. I was very willing to go. Obviously, that did not happen, but perhaps the miracles were happening and I could not see them because of the enormity of my grief. In time, I read that our loved ones benefit from our prayers, so I prayed for Scott. I wanted him to be well taken care of . . . and *well loved*.

I did not attend church after Scott died. I considered it at times, wondering if I would find the peace that I longed for, but never went. I trusted God knew where I was and would listen to me on my wonderful walks in the woods just as well as if I sat in a church pew. I felt closer to him in the woods than anywhere else.

I believe we all have to determine what helps us when we are struggling. Rabbi Harold Kushner, a bereaved father who wrote *When Bad Things Happen To Good People* (New York: Avon Books, 1981), said that many of us often have to "reconstruct" a new faith. In doing so, we hold on to new beliefs that are helpful and discard those that are not. Although this is not easy to accomplish while we are grieving, if we actually take the steps toward these new beliefs, we are also taking steps toward healing.

What is our role in all of this? To SEARCH! We are all searching for avenues of comfort, peace, and healing. It's part of both our grief journey and our spiritual journey. We each must choose our own path—no one else can do it for us—and that takes courage. We need to find what brings us a sense of inner peace. I read many, many books while trying to sort things out and find my own belief system. I also had the encouragement and guidance of Jane, my wonderful counselor who supported my search.

My journey through grief was difficult and challenging, but the reward for *not giving up* is that I now have a spiritual belief system which has finally brought me that seemingly elusive sense of peace. It took me quite a while to find my spirituality. It was a lot of hard work and I had to dig deep inside of myself to learn to trust again, but it has been so worthwhile. I can now see the *miracle* of life and death, not just the pain, and with that comes a much greater connection with God. I know I can nourish my soul's growth by the choices I make, like finding a church that fills my needs, reading about different religions or spirituality, or reaching out to others who are on similar quests. We each have our own unique soul journey and *everything* we do is for our soul's growth. At last, I know we are not victims in this life, but we experience and grow from the difficult times—and that is part of the journey.

I talk to Scott all the time, and I am certain that I will see him again. I also know I'm *still here* for a reason. I've accepted that, knowing my soul's journey did not end when Scott died . . . nor did his. Life goes on and on and on, and whether we are here or there, we are very much connected to one another at a soul level. I love knowing that! I believe in life after death, that Scott's death was a part of his soul plan, and that my life has an important plan too. It finally all makes sense to me.

The differences between religion and spirituality for everyone are as unique as each person is. As a newly bereaved mother, I found it difficult to trust any belief system. I questioned everything, and I see now that I *needed* to. Through those questions and the search, I was able to gain the understanding, knowledge, trust, faith, and strength to believe in life again, in God, in love, and in myself. My belief in spirituality has brought me a peace within that I probably would never have known. I'm truly grateful for this leg of my journey.

2

Creating Relationships With Your Spiritual Companions

When we look toward creating relationships with our spiritual companions, a two-pronged approach is often helpful. The first prong involves our spiritual companions who have crossed over, our angels and spirit guides, least of all not to forget God. The second prong involves our spiritual companions who are still earthbound. The purpose of this chapter is to help you see the importance of these two spiritual connections and how each of these relationships is invaluable to your life.

Forming connections with our spiritual companions on the Other Side at a time when we're so frantic and new in our grief can be challenging, difficult, and even disappointing. We yearn for a connection so badly, yet we've never known or done anything like it before. Communicating with our spiritual companions is not a topic that is openly or freely spoken about among relatives and friends, and certainly not throughout our society. As a newly bereaved mom who was fairly unaware of after-death communications, Sara never really knew such contact could occur without the help of a "medium." She desperately wanted to communicate with Scott but, like so many others who have lost loved ones, it was a totally new concept for her. Not knowing what to expect, Sara questioned whether she had any ability at all to connect with someone who had died. It was "so far out," she would say, yet she wanted to believe with all her heart that it was possible. Jane gently encouraged her to seek that connection with Scott. She knew how helpful it would be for Sara to believe that her beloved son's spirit still existed. Sara needed to understand that Scott had not just disappeared, but was now in spirit form on the Other Side and able to communicate in a whole new way. Once Sara learned that Scott was working and experimenting with his communication abilities on the Other Side, it brought her a wonderful new sense of peace and understanding. This knowledge encouraged her to become much more open to the messages that Scott was sending her.

Signs from Scott had shown Sara that he was out there. She had received a sign from him the day after his funeral that absolutely shocked her. She found a wondrous poem in an unexpected place and knew, without a doubt, it could only be from Scott. "In an instant, Scott grabbed my heart in an all new way and it was exhilarating! *I wanted more*!" " How," she wondered, "can I make those connections happen? I want them, I *need* them."

She begged for dreams, messages, and signs, but believed they all had to come through Scott. Would she have to *wait* forever? These special messages did not come as often as this desperate mother wanted, and Sara mourned for the added distance that she felt the timing put between her and Scott.

When Jane and Sara began working on her spiritual connection with Scott, they started with relaxation and meditation exercises. Unfortunately, Sara found it difficult to relax, and therefore meditate. This is common for grieving people. Relaxation is illusive, and the process of trying to gain this state is often frustrating. Some grievers perceive their inability to relax, and therefore to meditate, as failure. Sara said that the chaos she experienced because of Scott's sudden death, coupled with her all-consuming grief, muddied her brain and kept her nerves raw. Many grieving people also endure increased anxiety because of the fear that, with each passing day, month, and year, their loved one will be farther away. They become frantic to hang on to their loved one and want to work to create a continuing relationship. Of course, they don't understand how this can happen or what they need to do to assimilate the loss of the old relationship and pursue the new, more powerful one.

Sometimes, when efforts to connect do not happen fast enough or often enough, grievers feel let down. They may question their loving connection, feel like a failure, or experience a host of other debilitating emotions. The combination of these negative feelings and intense grief can cause grieving people to create new ways of coping that may not be in their best interest. Sara unknowingly created many such coping mechanisms. She became resistant to change and believed that, if nothing changed, she could keep Scott close. Because of this inner turmoil, she made a conscious decision to have everything remain the same. But, that didn't work either! After the death of a loved one, *everything* is different so nothing can remain the same. The more we resist, the more the chaos persists.

Of course, resistance is a common grief reaction. The control that is taken away by a sudden or unexpected death creates a need to find something—anything—in life to control. Some grievers come to counseling with an openness to whatever the counselor suggests. Others are convinced that they know what they need to do and, even when surviving loved ones and professionals point out that their way of coping is not to their benefit, the advice is resisted. Sara remembers a time when Jane suggested that she begin to form a new relationship with Scott. Let's just say that it wasn't a quiet and calm counseling session! Neither did Sara understand nor did she *want* to have a different kind of relationship with her son. She was adamant that she would not let go of the old relationship, and that she and Jane would have to work within those parameters.

Another obstacle for Sara was that she had a strong fear of seeing or hearing someone from another realm, even though she wanted so badly to keep hold of her relationship with Scott. Sara was virtually paralyzed by apprehension about trying something new and different, about letting go of old beliefs, and maybe even about gaining the new relationship. All of these fears are common. Unfortunately, the ghost stories we heard in childhood come back and cause us to think and act from a fear base instead of a faith and spiritual base.

Society plays a huge part in the belief structures of grieving people. Grievers have often said that family members and friends have suggested, and even expected, that they move on, get over their grief, and rejoin society. Grieving people are supposed to return to the way that they were before the loss occurred. These family members and friends are not being mean or cruel. They love the griever and want them to get back to normal. Many people have found that numerous friends and family members find it difficult to walk with them when they are in such pain, especially if the nongrievers believe that they cannot help to solve this problem.

This feeling of ostracism by society creates a need for some grieving people to separate themselves from family and friends. Another isolation factor is that grievers are not allowed to feel comfortable in sharing the signs they receive from their loved one with people who just plain don't want them to be grieving. Unfortunately, this separation and isolation prevents grieving people from gaining the support that they need and which, for many, is imperative.

Yet another negative by-product of resistance is that it inhibits the ability to feel and develop self-love. Sara remembers that her grief was also complicated by this factor. She saw her self-confidence, self-esteem, and self-knowledge diminish to a very low point. She had difficulty understanding the need to love and honor herself. She said, "I had unknowingly created a resistance to self-esteem and self-guidance. I had lost these two important and powerful self-help mechanisms because of my fervent quest to find Scott. I couldn't understand why the confidence I had as a mother didn't transform so that I would be able to hear and connect with my child after death." Of course, this complication is common in other grieving people too. However, it's important to understand that self-empowerment is necessary in order to do the work of making loving connections.

Feeling like a failure during the grieving process is a terrible burden to add to the mix of emotions that already consume anyone who has suffered a great loss. Everyone tries to cope in their own way. When we cannot see our future with any clarity or hope, we often fight the reality of life and death and how our roles have changed. We can unknowingly sabotage ourselves with our own thoughts and actions.

The great need that grievers have for something to believe in becomes more obvious as time passes. When the grip of grief begins to lessen its hold, many will require a new belief system that can support the intense desire of achieving a different relationship with their loved one as well as lessen the fears, anger, and guilt that have been stowaways along with the grief. Jane certainly encouraged Sara toward this new belief system, but Sara was so unsure of herself that she was afraid to try it.

Sara wanted others to see her and know her as a grieving mother. Many grievers feel that they have lost their identity as a mother, a spouse, a sibling, or a child after the death of a loved one. This is a frightening experience and it can complicate the grief process. Sara thought that, if others would acknowledge her as a grieving mother, she would have yet another way to hold on to Scott and her identity as Scott's mom. She now realizes that this desire created a major roadblock and that it was not a healthy place for her. It did not do anything to aid in her grief process, and certainly accomplished nothing toward helping her connect with Scott and live a more spiritual life.

Grieving people are best served when they can understand the necessity to do the internal work of processing all the grief and preparing to "hear" their deceased loved one. Many times, this need comes as a surprise because grievers believe they have already been doing all the internal work necessary to assimilate their loss. Even those who have engaged in counseling from the start of the grieving process, have reinvested in life, and have been altruistic find that doing this internal work is helpful and necessary to living a spiritual life. Sara told Jane, "I believed I was healing and living a fairly normal life, which included adjusting to my new relationship with Scott. After all, didn't internal work mean trying to mend my broken heart?"

"Not exactly," Jane said. "Assimilating Scott's death into every aspect of your life is the real internal work. That means looking at the most difficult situations you have pushed away and assimilating Scott's death into those."

Sara pondered the words "most difficult situations." She wondered if Jane meant the situations she had avoided, the ones she didn't want to talk about, or the ones she hadn't dealt with because she knew they would have hurt too much. Sara thought that Jane probably was speaking about those circumstances. She had to be, didn't she?

All of these roadblocks unknowingly prevent grieving people from the greater connections with their loved one that they crave. Looking back now, at each one of these roadblocks, Sara can see that she prevented herself from being open to more of a connection. Sara had to find her way back from the depths of grief, and then let a lot of things go, see other things in a new light, or just plain change them altogether. Fortunately, most of these obstacles are not problematic for Sara anymore because she has worked through them to get to where she is today. It's like the old saying, "the more you want something, the harder you'll work." It was hard work, it *is* hard work, but the outcome is so worth it. Sara didn't tackle all of these issues at the same time because that would have been impossible. She tried to deal with each roadblock as it arose, one tiny step at a time. Her road looks a lot clearer now and, accordingly, the gate for greater communication with Scott has opened. Grief, they say, is a great teacher. Sara now understands that beyond a doubt.

Everyone who is grieving and searching for answers can face roadblocks to that much-desired communication with their loved one. Understand that the obstacles you face might delay your communication, but don't give up. Believe it or not, we can learn from those obstacles! This kind of work is heart based and it's worth every challenge to create that spiritual relationship with your loved one.

Why connections may not happen.

- Connections sometimes don't happen as we expect or hope.
- A loved one may have had a troubled existence on Earth and therefore, may have had a traumatic exit from Earth.
- A loved one may have behaved on Earth and created emotional or

physical pain for others.
- It may be too early to make this connection.
- You may try to reach a loved one who has died a long time ago.
- Our loved ones don't want to create dependencies.
- Of course there are other explanations why this may have been a difficult or frustrating process for you. We haven't covered all the many reasons here. We hope that the following information will be helpful in having a continuing relationship with your loved one.

Most grieving people want to connect with their deceased loved one. Many believe that their loved one is out there—in heaven or on the Other Side. When educated about signs, numerous grievers have related stories about receiving these loving connections through signs and messages from their loved one. Unfortunately, they don't know how to encourage this communication. They have run out of energy because they are using every bit of it just to breathe and function in a world that feels hostile and foreign. This lack of energy, and for some their persistence in keeping things the same, can unknowingly set up the barricades and roadblocks to the spiritual connections that we talked about above. This is what Sara experienced and what she is now working tirelessly to prevent from happening to others.

Concerns about what others think about after-death communication can create even more obstacles for those who are grieving. Those who are lucky find support through understanding families, counselors, and groups. When grieving people have this support, they are better able to investigate the different types of loving connections and find the one that most fits their needs. Unfortunately, many in our society are not receptive to the signs and messages from loved ones. Grievers are excited to share these experiences that prove their loved one truly is not gone, but their words fall on deaf ears. They have to remain cautious and vigilant to protect their fragile state of mind. It's important for society to meet grievers where they are and support the beliefs that will help them the most.

So, as grieving people, where do we gather our information about after-death communications? Many people think spirituality is about crystal balls and Ouija boards . . . and that it's dark and scary too. Unfortunately, mediums, even reputable and gifted ones are often perceived as kooks, and are debunked time and again by the skeptics. But, grievers need proof of communication with, and sometimes even sightings of, loved ones who have died. They need to trust in what feels right—whatever that is—even if it is impossible to gain through conventional means.

Some organized religions teach that spiritual communication is evil and should not be believed. Those who voice this doctrine are not silent in their views. This can be disconcerting to people who are grieving the loss of a loved one. They often wonder where God is in all of this, and ask, "Would God allow my loved one to communicate with me directly, or not? Should I try?"

Grieving people find it hard to have faith in much of anything. They wonder if they can even trust what others have told them about the communications they received when their loved ones died. They ponder whether they can or should trust mediums and intuitives. They are reluctant to have confidence in anything because they don't want to set their hearts up to be broken again.

Many grieving people expect to hear their loved ones say, "Hi," in the same sweet familiar voice they had when in physical form. When this doesn't happen, grievers are at a loss about how to make this loving connection. Many believe that only people with psychic powers can communicate with those who have died. This is not correct, and this book will help you understand that reality.

It is also very important to create relationships with our spiritual companions who are still earthbound (that is, other living people here on Earth). As you walk the course that Sara and other grievers do as described above, you will want to talk about your new path. You will need a safe environment so that you can ask questions and express your thoughts and emotions. All too quickly, you'll discover that your next-door neighbor or even your best friend will raise an eyebrow at your newfound topic of conversation. Because of this, it is imperative that you seek a support system that nurtures you. As you grow spiritually, those who are close to you may start to have a hard time accepting your new path. Understandably, other people are scared of domains that they don't understand and happenings that they can't control.

In this book, we concentrate on growing spiritually through grief. However, once you start walking down your spiritual path, you will find that it becomes quite addictive. You will start putting pieces of your life into place and viewing the world through different eyes. It will be enriching, invigorating, and scary—all at the same time. Initially, you may start to read books about others who have found their way on this path. You may also want to try the meditation and imagery that we highly recommend. You may discover groups of other people who have similar interests and are also walking a spiritual path. Joining a church that has a spiritual, with or without a religious, focus can be helpful too. At some point, you may want to attend a Zen or Buddhist retreat to learn more about their ways. The path won't be easy. If you are married and your spouse is not into these new perspectives, he or she might find going to a Zen retreat threatening in some way. As you bring new forms of thought back home with you, it can frighten your family. When we start to think differently, we upset the apple cart.

On the other hand, you may find it hard to break away from ingrained thoughts that you have been taught since childhood. Your intuition may be pulling you in a new direction, but your old patterns of thought may be stopping you from moving forward. Not wanting to go against your family and religion is a difficult place to be in. This is another good reason to participate in a support group. There, you can form relationships with spiritual companions—people just like yourself—who will listen to you and share how they overcame obstacles in their paths. Hearing their stories will help you make strident steps forward. As you walk this journey, you will be surprised by things that will come up about yourself. When your "shadow side" surfaces, you may not like all of the components of yourself. For example, you may have been raised a "secret racist" where the family denies it verbally, but their actions and comments scream "racist." You may find that, even though you were raised in this way and agree with the racist viewpoint to some degree, it is not something that works for your life now. This is but one paradigm of many to come.

So, how do you meet your earthbound spiritual companions? There are many ways to become acquainted with people who have the same interests and can be of support to you. You can attend a workshop like ours, join a study group, take meditation or yoga classes, or get in touch with the Association for Research and Enlightenment (A.R.E.) in your local area. You can even take a metaphysical class on the Internet where you can maintain your anonymity and still meet people globally who are moving in the same direction. This is an exciting time of exploration into "you." We want to make sure that you receive all the support and encouragement you can at this sensitive crossroads in your life. Be sure to look for and take any opportunity to increase your spiritual awareness and ability to network with spiritual companions who have similar interests.

GRIEF RELIEF

3

Making Connections That Count

The slap, slap, slap of the windshield wipers droned on. The spray from the roadway made a shushing sound under the tires of my gold Taurus. The backseat was filled with boxes of mascara, blush, eye liner, and lipstick. Cosmetics had lost their allure for me but I needed the job of delivering these items to the department stores across my territory.

It always seemed to be gray when I serviced this store which was about an hour away from my home. Today's cold weather and off and on rain showers added to my depression and the weariness in my soul. My whole body seemed to be screaming in agony, missing my son, Scott, and wondering how I could continue to force myself to do this menial task when my sweet son had died.

Being alone, in my car, was usually a place of solace and peace for me. I didn't have to talk with anyone. I never played the radio anymore, never sang, never even talked to myself. Somehow, the complete quiet was preferable over any noise at all. It's not that this silence took my grief away or even made it better. It's just that everything seemed like noise to me and this prevented me from using every ounce of concentration I had available to think about my Scott.

Today, however, was different. A friend had sent me a cassette tape of one song, "One Sweet Day" by Mariah Carey and Boyz II Men. I listened to this song over and over again all during my travel time. When I allowed myself to listen to music, I spent the time looking for something in the song that might give me some hope that Scott was sending me a message. I wasn't getting any message. It was a nice song, but with the gray Ohio day certainly "no sun was shining down on me," as the song's refrain suggested.

There is a big bridge that I had to go over to get to this particular store. I had gone over it many times since Scott had died. I would always say to myself, "God do it today! Let a truck run in to me because I can't stand this any longer. God just put me out of my misery. I don't want to cause an accident, I don't want to hurt anyone else but just let it happen to me." On this day, nearly a year after Scott's death, my plea was even more fervent. I was tired and ready to go home. However, it was not to be.

On the way back home from this store, I was again listening to this cassette. I was just hoping to feel that zing that Scott was inside my heart or communicating with me. I had heard this was possible so I spent my days hoping and begging for it to happen for me. As I continually listened, I began to slowly feel that there might be something I had been missing. I turned up the volume to cut out the rain and the road noise and listened even more intently. I began to think that somebody else, perhaps the writer of this song, felt something that I felt and could identify with. It seemed that the words to this song were beginning to sink into my slow and depressed brain and were actually talking to me.

I began to ponder how these lyrics might be relating to Scott. Although it was still totally gray outside and pouring down rain, just as the song said, "and I know you're shining down on me from Heaven" I felt, not heard, but felt someone tell me to look up and to the left. I was shocked! I spotted a perfectly round circle in the clouds and through this circle I could see incredible blue sky and the sun directly in the center. I was stunned! I looked to the other side of me and it was gray, I looked back again and it was still there. I was looking everywhere, front and back, side to side, everywhere, nothing but battleship gray skies. I looked back again, up and to the left, and there it was! It was STILL there. I then knew this had to be from Scott because it was too incredible and too amazing to just be happening in the sky at the exact same time as the song was playing those words!

When this happened for me, it opened up the possibility that Scott could indeed send me a message and I could receive it. I had yearned and wanted a sign so badly. I had been trying to make signs happen that would assure me that Scott was still with me in some way, and I had found that wishing was not going to make them happen. I told Scott everyday that I wanted a sign because I knew that it could happen. My faith assured me he was there, that he existed and could do magical things. This experience proved to me that he could send me a sign and I needed to continue to have faith in my son and be patient.

I was especially excited because that afternoon I had an appointment with Jane. I told her what had happened, about the song that was given to me and about my trip on this incredibly gray day. I explained how beautiful the circle was and how incredible the sun had been positioned directly in the center of this perfect sphere. I told her I knew it had to be from Scott. She listened to my story and asked, "Do you think that Scott might have been telling you that it was your SON instead of the SUN shining down on you?" I was so excited that I cried for joy. I was even more excited and grateful to Scott for giving me this new message. It was so personal and meant the world to me. Now when I listen to that song, I know for me the words are that my SON is shining down on me!

It was important for my survival to believe Scott could continue to connect with me. I had read books about what other people had experienced and I wanted those things to happen. Jane talked to me about these beliefs and supported me in knowing that if I felt a connection with Scott was important to my well-being she would work to help me identify loving connections. Now I not only believe it, I can attest to it.

I began telling people of my experience, I didn't care what they said, and I did NOT care if they believed me. My telling them wasn't to convince them of what I knew to be true. I was just sharing my experience with others. This feeling of not having to prove my beliefs lifted a weight off my shoulders and allowed me to focus on what was beneficial in my own grief process. Jane always told me that there was no right or wrong way to grieve; it was just my way. I was figuring that out and it was a painful and slow journey. Simply sharing my story was an important part of my grief process.

This wonderful message from Scott has given me great hope. It caused me to take a big jump, no really a huge leap in my grief work. Scott died while being trained to work at a national park in Colorado. He developed a seizure disorder when he was fifteen, but it was controlled with medication. Unfortunately, when he arrived in Colorado, he was diagnosed with strep throat. The altitude combined with a high fever, and his seizure disorder created a recipe for disaster and his death.

I wanted to believe that he didn't just disappear that one May 20th and that he would never be heard from again. I wanted to believe that he knew where I was and he knew where to put the sun in the sky so that I would see it. I wanted to believe that the music was brought to me for this purpose. This connection has opened up all kinds of new thought processes for me that help me look toward the future instead of only at the past. (Jane Bissler & Lisa Heiser, *Loving Connections: The Healing Power of After Death Communications*, in press).

The story you have just read shows what loving connections can provide for a griever. Learning how to make these connections is only part of the task and, in our opinion, not the most important chore. *Being open to these connections* is our true responsibility and, although this sounds easy, it is not.

We all have an innate need to feel connected with our loved ones. If the hard work of connection is not done, that hole is *never* filled. Some try to fill the gap by eating, shopping, drinking, smoking, or working too much, but the emptiness remains. And, many do this out of fear.

For those who are grieving, fear is a normal emotional response that results in feelings of anxiety. While grieving the death of a loved one, fear comes into play in several different ways. First, when the loved one is no longer around, fear can be felt as a result of personal safety issues. More importantly, after the death of a loved one, fear results from the realization that we will not be physically connected with our loved one during this lifetime. When this fact becomes a reality, anxiety resulting from fear occurs.

Sara put to words an expression common in grieving people, "I was amazed at how much fear I unknowingly carried with me." Normalizing this fear is important work, and making loving connections is an excellent way to extinguish this fear.

Sometimes, fear comes about when we don't trust ourselves. Trusting ourselves to be able to live without our loved one is difficult. Learning to trust in life, in God or a Higher Power, and in our own abilities to function are other trust issues that challenge us at the beginning of the grieving process. Unfortunately, fear not only is energy draining, but it is energy blocking. Fear robs the body of needed power to get through life's normal ups and downs. Fear also stands as a concrete wall blocking the recognition of signs given to us by our loved one. Meditation and deep relaxation can help tear down this wall. It might seem that this sets up a contrary situation: energy is needed to open up the channels, but the fear consumes the energy needed to do this very thing. Just be patient with yourself and know that your loved one is patient and will send you signs as you work toward this connection.

Loving connections happen when your heart, your mind, and your body are all in sync. As Louise Hay writes in *Heal Your Body* (Carlsbad, CA: Hay House, 1984, p.7) our minds have the power to create dis-ease. Sara bore witness to this when she said, "I suffered with terrible headaches for twenty-five years. I now know I can get a raging headache when my thoughts do not agree with what my heart really knows. For me, there was a disconnect between what my heart knew to be true and the fear I was creating with my thoughts."

She continued, "I truly understand now that my heart and soul are pure goodness and my thoughts, when filled with worry, fear, and anger, equal a bad connection, and thus a headache. It is a physical sign that lets me know I need to pay attention to my thoughts . . . the negative thoughts. I have learned the hard way, that worry is pointless, it's wasted energy."

Through counseling, Sara learned that the fear, anxiety, and anger were building the concrete wall between her heart and Scott's heart, and between her soul and Scott's soul. Sara, like many others, is a natural at fear and worry. She works hard, daily, to give this up so that she can be constantly connected with the love of her life, Scott. Sara said, "I will literally force myself—using deep breathing, calling a friend, going for a walk, talking to Scott and asking for his help, reminding myself that I can control those negative thoughts— to STOP the fear and worry within. My connection with Scott means far more to me than those thoughts! Scott does not work with negativity . . . he's pure *love* and, to be in soul-to-soul connection with him, I must be also!"

We need to be fully aware of how powerful our thoughts are. In grief, our pain, anger, fear, doubt, and guilt can create tons of negativity and fear. We have to work to eliminate that or it will rob us of the very energy we require to survive, and to be continually and lovingly connected to our loved one. By doing that hard work, we'll begin to unblock the emotions that prevent the loving connections we so desire.

So, what are these connections? Bill and Judy Guggenheim wrote the book *Hello From Heaven* (New York: Bantam, 1997). In this book, they reviewed 3,300 connection stories from interviewees and created twelve separate categories of connections. We present the categories to you here to help you know what to open yourself up to, what to pay attention to, and what to actively look for.

- Sensing a Presence (p.23) -- This is feeling the presence of your loved one, a very real physical sensation. Have you ever felt that someone is behind you, only to discover when you turn around that no one is there? This is the feeling described in this category.

- Hearing a Voice (p.35) —Some hear an audible voice through their ears. This is somewhat rare, however. There is also a telepathic or mental type of communication that is heard internally, like intuition. People describe this as a thought popping into their head. They know It's not their thought, but they try to make a convincing argument that it is. Sara heard the words, "Bloom where you are planted," referring to the need to accept her life as a now-childless mother, and to grow or "bloom" from that experience. She has done a wonderful job with this task requested by her son, Scott.

- Feeling a Touch (p.51)—This is felt as a soft breeze or touch, or as a comforting arm around your shoulder. Many people say it feels like a feather touching your cheek. Sometimes this touch comes while sleeping at night. It might feel like pressure on the side or the end of the bed. Others feel a soft breeze when no breeze is apparent to anyone else in the room.

- Smelling a Fragrance (p.62)—This is a relatively common type of communication. Usually this scent is one that is familiar to you or one that is somehow connected to your loved one. It may be the aroma of perfume, cologne, or even tobacco. Carole described, "I walked into Paul's bathroom and was overpowered by the sent of his cologne. There was no cologne of his in this bathroom or anywhere in our house. It was unmistakably Paul's cologne."

- Partial Appearances (p.76)—Partial appearances are one of the rarest types of connections. They are comprised of a loved one showing their legs and feet or head and shoulders. They can also appear as a shadow. Sharon saw Stephanie's sweet smiling face above her headstone at the cemetery. Jane has experienced this type of a connection with a client, Dick, whom she helped as he was dying. He appeared at the end of the hallway at her office. There was no doubt about who this was, not necessarily by his appearance because she only saw his legs and feet, but by his energy. It was also clear that he came to thank her for helping him while he was alive.

- Full Appearances (p.94)—This is the rarest of all connections. In this connection, you will see the entire person. Their body looks absolutely solid and real. This often happens at twilight or dawn, but not when you are in a dream state. John woke up to see his beautiful wife standing at the end of their bed in the teal dress they had both loved. She looked young and healthy even though her body had been ravaged by ALS.

- A Glimpse Beyond (p.112)—This is seeing the place or consciousness that your loved one sees. It can be a vivid and colorful view. These visions can take place in meditation, during a guided imagery, or while in deep prayer. Joanie saw her daughter, Susie, sitting on a park bench surrounded by the family pets who had also died. It was vibrant and real. Although it appeared that Susie didn't know that Joanie was seeing her, it brought peace to Joanie to know what Susie was doing and how she looked.

- Encounters at Twilight (p.128)—These encounters usually occur at twilight or dusk when you would be in a half awake, half asleep state. These connections can be a sense of, or a touch from, your loved one. Carlie felt a hand on her shoulder just before her alarm went off one morning. She felt confident that this was her grandfather wishing her well on a day full of exams.

- Dream Visits (p.142)—Dream visits are different from dreams. They are more vivid, colorful, and unforgettable. One way to ascertain the difference between a dream and a connection that comes through a dream is that, if there is interaction between you and your loved one, it's usually a visit. It is easier for our loved ones to reach us in the sleep state when we are more relaxed and our energies are more open. Mike has visits from his wife, Laura, where he feels her kisses and her touch. Another example of this interaction is Bonnie's loving connection with her sister. Bonnie saw her sister in the distance and approached her. Together they chatted while walking down a path that seemed to be heaven to Bonnie.

Bonnie recalled the incredible beauty of the vivid colors, the entire conversation, and the way her sister looked even though this dream visit took place years ago.

- Out of Body (p.164)—This is probably the most frightening connection for people to experience because the sensation is so unique. While sleeping, or sometimes while in deep meditation, you may feel as if you have left your body and traveled to another realm. Dale experiences this type of connection regularly. He finds that he can look down and see himself sleeping. He then "travels" to another plane where he sees his deceased sons and spouse. It's important to realize that you are absolutely safe when this happens. Your angels or guides will be traveling with you, even though you might not see or feel their presence.

- Telephone Calls (p.182)—Many people have this connection, but think that it's a solicitor or wrong number. Sometimes these calls are that, but oftentimes they are a loving connection. With this type of connection, the telephone actually rings. You may hear nothing on the line or you may hear the voice of your loved one when you answer. Either way, consider this as a loving connection and know that, whether or not you heard it, your loved one was saying,

"Hi!" and "I'm OK!"

- Physical Phenomena (p.195)—These are often the loving connections that are most sought after. It's important to understand that our loved ones have an ability to "mess with" electrical and electronic devices. Soul energy, without being slowed down with the human body, runs very fast. The speed of electricity is slow comparatively, but is closer to soul energy than other energy sources here on Earth. Therefore, our soul's connection to electricity is strong and allows our loved ones to manipulate its flow. Roxana's dad sends her "hellos" through the streetlights. They go on and off as she passes under them.

    Other physical phenomena could be through pictures being moved, messages appearing on computer screens, or through natural phenomena like rainbows appearing. Sandi experienced a message that came through the Caller ID systems of people she called. Her deceased daughter's name showed up when Sandi made the calls. It happened for about a month and was assurance to her that her sweet daughter lives on and mother and daughter remain lovingly connected.

Receiving these signs and promoting continuing relationships is what our book is all about. Signs and loving connections are a way not only to help you survive the pain of grief and loss, but to thrive and live life in a way that allows you to experience all that your soul needs and wants. Grieving is so hard. The pain and agony that comes from missing your loved one and yearning for them takes so much of your daily energy. Knowing that these signs exist, and working toward your openness to them, is a helpful way to assimilate the loss you feel so that you can truly believe in life again.

GRIEF RELIEF

4

Meditation and Imagery

When people hear the word "meditation," they usually get tense, which is ironic because meditation is meant to help us become de-stressed and reach more spiritual planes of existence. Whether working with people individually or in a group, we always asks what it is that causes each of them to not be able to meditate. Every time, the same few answers arise.

- I can't sit still.
- I've tried to meditate before, but I can't keep my concentration.
- My body hurts sitting like this for so long.
- I know I should meditate like this (whatever *this* is), but I can't.

Our response is simple: Let's forget all about the "shoulds" of meditation.

First of all, sit any way you like—on a chair, laying down, legs crossed, whatever is most comfortable for you and your body. Let's face it, most of us are either out of shape or have aches and pains from an injury or arthritis.

So, what works for one of us, won't work for another. We were not born sitting in a lotus position (sometimes called cross legged or Indian style), so to try and start there seems a little ridiculous. Maybe, if you want to eventually get to the lotus position, you can work toward it slowly when you are *not* trying to meditate.

The next question is keeping your concentration, but don't worry about this. Whenever you find that your mind is wandering, just concentrate on your breathing. (You can use the breathing technique explained in the Breath Work section below.)

Many of us have an idea in our mind that meditation has to look a certain way for it to be successful. We have a picture of a guru in a lotus position sitting under a tree. But, that is an illusion. Being able to sit still is not a requirement for meditation. Again, being able to sit for long periods of time does not a professional meditator make. If we put out to the universe that we want to meditate, we will. The key is *listening*, and each of us listens in our own unique ways.

We are not all born to do everything the same way, so why should we put meditation into a box either? You can do a moving meditation while you take a walk, or pull the weeds in the garden, or dance around your apartment. There are many ways to meditate.

You may even find, as you practice the walking meditation, that your mind and body do become still for one minute, and that minute may then turn into five, ten, and so on. We need to be kind to ourselves and take baby steps instead of berating ourselves like the rest of society does at times. When we criticize ourselves, we act counter intuitively and lose harmony with our Higher Power.

Next, we need to think about a few fundamental steps both before and after meditation.

Before Meditation

1. **Set your intention.** You always want to make sure you say, "I want to connect to the highest level of truth that there Is" (or your own variation on that intention) before you start your meditation.

2. **Set an ideal.** This is a thought or an idea to think about and focus on while meditating. For the beginner, we suggest concentrating on your breathing (see the Breath Work and Imagery sections below).

3. **Choose a time and place for daily meditation.** Be regular, consistent, and patient! It takes time to develop a

routine. Once you begin to get the feel for meditation, you can meditate anywhere and at any time. You will be able to reach a place of serenity and peace just by doing some deep breathing and focusing on releasing your stress. (This is a great tool for which to strive.)

4. **Create a sacred space.** Choose a place for your meditation space that is quiet and calm, and where you can immediately feel at peace. For example, choose a favorite chair with a table next to it where you can keep your journals and music. When you sit there, you will immediately begin by taking a deep breath and start to feel relaxed even if you are not meditating.

5. **Ask for guidance and connection.** Ask your loved ones, your God, Creator, or Supreme Being, or however you understand the universal life force, for guidance and wisdom. You may pose a simple question like, "What am I to understand?" and you may hear an answer from a spirit guide, angel, or a loved one in Spirit.

After Meditation

6. **Offer a prayer of gratitude.** Offer a prayer from your faith or tradition or a prayer you create to express gratitude for the many gifts you have been given.

7. **Make sure to dedicate your meditation and prayers to whoever you believe in.** (For instance, you may want to dedicate yours to all living beings, that they may be free from suffering.)

8. **Journal.** You may want to keep a journal beside your meditation space to write in when you have finished. You may write how long you were able to meditate, or a consistent thought or vision of a person who kept coming to mind. You will find a journal to be very helpful in charting your progress.

Breath Work

Breath work is extremely important when you are meditating. It helps to relieve stress in the body and, at the same time, keeps your mind empty and focused. When you start to lose your concentration or feel as if your mind is wandering, just come back to your breathing technique. It will re-center you. Sometimes if your mind is constantly wandering off to a particular idea, thought, or person, there may be something you need to be aware of. It may be that your mind is turned off enough to the noise of the world to let something from your intuitive side come through. As you become more familiar with yourself during meditation, you will be more able to delineate the difference between what is important and what is not important.

The Tibetan Breathing Technique has been around for ages. Deneene learned it long ago from a monk who was teaching a relaxation and meditation class at a local monastery. You can also find techniques that are similar in most Eastern meditation rituals (for example, the benefits and the circulatory effects of breathing deep). Let's begin.

1. You may want to get out your journal to keep track of your breathing techniques.

2. You need to get yourself in a comfortable position, whatever that may be, in your sacred place. (Even a chair in the kitchen is fine.)

3. You need to understand about human lungs. We have two different sections in our lungs: an upper and a lower portion. These two sections work with our bodies in completely different ways to bring oxygen to our organs and systems. Most of us are chest breathers, meaning that we breathe from

our mouths to fill up the upper portion of our lungs. The upper portion is connected to our autonomic nervous system that gives the "fight or flight" response. Therefore, this type of breathing actually causes ourselves and our bodies undo stress.

Our lower lungs, which are connected to nose breathing, are just the opposite. Breathing deeply through the nose simulates a relaxation response that tells our bodies that all is right within our world and we are safe. The best way to know if you are breathing with the lower lobes of your lungs is to place your hand on your stomach and feel it rise with your breath. This can be accomplished by mouth breathing, but it is much harder to do so.

Don't be shocked that you have never done this before. Many people do not have this knowledge. Most of the people who know the differences in breathing are either singers or athletes. Now that you know the differences, you can see why breathing with your lower lungs is beneficial to meditation.

So, take a moment and play around with your breathing. Take a few breaths into your mouth just to fill up your chest, then exhale through your mouth. Now, take a few breaths from your nose, push your stomach out, then exhale through your mouth again. Can't you feel the difference?

Which way of breathing makes you feel calmer?

Now, inhale through your nose, push your stomach out while keep your hand on it, and hold your breath for five seconds if you can. You will want to work up to fifteen seconds a breath but, for now, five seconds will be great. You may feel your heart pound in your chest while you hold your breath or even feel your ears pulse. This is normal. Your body will become accustomed to you holding your breath.

While you are exhaling, feel the stress come out of your fingertips and toes.

Next, put the book down and, for about five minutes, do some more playing with your breathing. If you can last longer than five minutes—great. Have fun getting to know your body and your breathing, and get lost in the relaxation.

- How did that feel?
- How long were you able to hold your breath?
- Were you able to do this breathing technique for more than five minutes while practicing?
- You may want to start journaling all of this, right now!

Most people find that this breathing technique helps them become very relaxed, and they end up doing it for longer than five minutes.

But, don't beat yourself up. You are who you are and it will all come with diligent practice, every day, once a week, whatever you set as your timeline. As long as you stick to that simple practice, or one of your own design, your breathing techniques will improve.

Imagery

Imagery is another truly wonderful tool. To name a few of its uses, it can be applied in many things like pain control, stress control, anger management, changing characteristics about ourselves, and having visitations with those who have crossed over.

But, let's take pain control. Deneene used this tool a lot with her hospice patients and also taught the technique to their family members. It is beneficial to use while medication is taking effect, or as a more natural approach to pain. Sometimes it helps if someone else guides a patient through this meditation if the pain is too intense. If you are the guide, make sure that you first have a conversation with the patient and ask details about the favorite place where they have been that makes them feel the most peaceful. Have the patient describe the setting and even the smell. For those of you who wish to use this technique for yourself, make sure that you call to mind a vivid memory of your favorite place before you begin. It will help bring you to a place of pain control quicker once the pain begins. Regardless of who you are helping (yourself or someone else), make sure that you follow these steps. Once you get the imagery meditation down, you can modify it to better fit you and your circumstances. First of all, the person who is being helped with pain must try to relax. Guide them by saying:

- Start by taking several deep breaths from your stomach.
- If you can close your eyes, go to a favorite place that is serene and beautiful where you feel very relaxed.
- Remember how that place makes you feel— visualize its surroundings, hear its sounds, and sense its smells.
- While you are sitting in this place of serenity, keep your eyes closed and take some deep breaths.
- Stay in this place and feel its serenity. You will come out of it naturally.
- If you are restless, remember your breathing and it will bring you quietly back to this place.

People who are in pain tend to breathe through their chest. They also breathe more rapidly and stiffen up. You will know when the meditation is working because the person's breathing will become slower and they will relax.

This technique can also be used for stress control or anger management.

Stress Control or Anger Management
- Breathe
- Close your eyes
- Go to a place where you feel serene.
- Smell, see, listen
- Let your body relax.
- Imagine yourself happy and content.
- Now, envision yourself in the situation that made you feel anxious.
- See the situation through these new eyes; come to it from a place of control and think about how you would like to see yourself handle the same situation differently.
- Breath deeply from your stomach.
- Envision the same scenario but, this time, use the new behavior pattern and play it out.

Changing Yourself

Changing yourself can include many things like helping with grief, weight loss, a new job, learning a new language, seeing yourself more spiritually, or being able to meditate. In fact, you can use this in any area of your life where you are having trouble and you'd like to improve or begin anew. It is great for making life changes such as seeing yourself go on with life again after a significant loss of a child, spouse, or companion animal. Or, beginning a career you have always wanted, or moving to a different climate or new part of the world. You should also read about the "power to create" in Chapter 9 and implement those suggestions here.

Perform this guided imagery if you are having trouble meditating:

- Breathe
- Close your eyes.
- Feel relaxed.
- Now, picture yourself in this new way (for example, being thinner, meditating, speaking a foreign language, living in a new place, working at your dream job).
- Actually visualize yourself performing these new actions or improving on the old ways.
- Observe yourself doing these actions with confidence and pride, and being successful in your new endeavor and doing it well.
- Smell, see, and hear people and things around you so that this new environment feels like it is real.
- You can perform this imagery anywhere and do it a couple of times a day or more until you can visualize it easily throughout your day.
- Now, take action and begin to do something that will point you in the new direction.
- Continue to create this new pattern in your life, forge ahead with your dream, and the rest will follow.

Meeting Loved Ones Who Have Crossed Over

- Breathe
- Imagine you are in a forest.
- You see a path illuminated with light.
- As you walk that path, you come out to a sunlit meadow.
- You feel the sun on your face, smell the grass, see the flowers and trees.
- This is a holy place, so feel the serenity.
- You look ahead and see someone coming over a hill bathed in warm sunlight.
- As that person gets closer, you realize it is your loved one.
- You can embrace
- You can smell your loved one.
- You can kiss your loved one.
- You can look in your loved one's eyes and say how much you miss them.
- You can hear your loved one talk to you.
- You can tell your loved one anything you need to say.
- After a while, your loved one will have to leave and you hug goodbye.
- You watch your loved one walk back up the hill in the sunlight.
- You know your loved one is safe and loved.
- You are comforted in knowing this is a place where you can always see and touch your loved one.

- You turn around feeling renewed by your time together and head down the path to the woods.

With all these new tools to choose from, you are on your way to creating a more peaceful and cohesive you. Meditation and imagery are effective only if you put them into action. If you do, you can begin to be more at peace and to focus on you.

Keep trying! It does take practice. If you aren't able to achieve the results you are hoping for, consult someone who can help you. For some people, meditation is more difficult than it is for others. Be patient with yourself and don't have unrealistic expectations.

5

It's a Sole/Soul Journey

There are actually two journeys in life:
the SOLE journey and the SOUL journey. What
are the differences between the ways that we
travel these two passages and how it impacts
our grief process?

The S-O-L-E Journey

In the S-O-L-E journey, we are referring
to the body we have been given, the lifetime
we are living, and the experiences we are
having and perceiving right now. You have the
free will to make your own choices and
decisions in this lifetime. As an individual, you
do the work, make the choices, and create the
thoughts *by* yourself *for* yourself. You own this
lifetime. The decisions and outcomes are your
own.

We make many of these decisions every
day without giving them much thought. But,
when the death of a loved one occurs, we are
suddenly thrown into a state of crisis. Even
though we do not feel emotionally able to do
so, we must continue to make decisions for our
sole journey. No one else can make our

decisions for us. Of course, we'd rather let someone else take over and decide what is best for us, but *no one can*. We are desperate for that support, because we feel weak, confused, and helpless. It is important for us to know that our family and friends *want* to make us feel better, but it's not their job. It is ours, because it is part of our sole journey.

Many people who suddenly find themselves struggling with grief have never given any thought to their sole/soul journey. That's understandable because people simply do not spend time and energy wondering about issues that are not presently causing them concern. Thoughts about how we will grieve do not come up until they are needed. Perhaps it would be helpful to do this work prior to its need, but it doesn't appear to be realistic.

When grief comes, you will have to ask yourself if you are going to walk the walk, or be carried. You each have to make that choice. You also must determine the roads that you will take. On this journey, you need to pay attention to the warning signs that your body is giving you. Are you going to heal or not? Will you choose to not eat and waste away? Or, will you eat too much, drink too much, or stay in bed all day? Will you seek counseling or support? Will you attend these appointments or meetings with an open mind? Will you take what is being said and see if it works? Will you listen and WANT it? Can you forgive someone who has hurt you, even if they don't seek your forgiveness?

These are all SOLE decisions. They are choices that must be made. However, we also must determine if they are good ones for us. Do we want to stay in the past where there is safety or see what the future holds? Of course, no one can answer that question. We learn by making both the good choices and the bad ones, and that is all part of the journey.

Thoughts are a key part of this decision-making process, because the thoughts are yours. You determine what to do with them. Remember, your thoughts create. It's Important to pay attention to that and create the positive. Fear creates failure. Exactly what are you creating with your thoughts when you decide to stay stuck in the same place, or play it safe and not move in a direction that will benefit you? Only you can change the way you think and act. Most grievers come to realize that it is through the ups and downs of grief, and through the pain and rewards of making decisions, that change and growth occurs. Some decisions are beneficial, and some are not. Owning them all as personal learning lessons helps a griever become stronger and more able to handle the changes that continue to occur.

This is the SOLE work: making our choices and following through with them. Will the choices you make help to fulfill your life's purpose? Will you challenge yourself? It's all for you, by you, and the only control you have is over yourself.

The S-O-U-L Journey

The S-O-U-L journey is beyond our physical and mental needs. Our soul is where love and goodness dwell within us, and where faith, patience, and courage are found. A soul is something that many believe is with us when we are born, and the one thing that leaves the physical body when we die. It carries the essence of who we are on to the next phase of eternal life. Our soul is the constant that remains the same and grows with our experiences and ever-changing perceptions. It is our spirit that is connected to God and everything around us. It is who we are from one lifetime or phase of existence to another, regardless of our sex, our race, and where or for how long we dwell in this universe.

But, when is our soul born? Where has it been before our physical birth? And, when will it cease to exist? Unfortunately, Jane, Sara, and Deneene do not have the answers to these questions. We do believe that our souls have always existed and will continue to exist for all eternity. We do believe that we are a part of a mass of energy that we call God. If our souls are a part of God, we are in essence all a part of each other.

Before we are born, pre-carnation, we believe we met with a council of angels who asked us what we want to accomplish on our journey to Earth, both for ourselves and for the humanity we are being born into. This is a critical period before our rebirth because it will contribute toward shaping the format our life will take during the time we are on this planet. We also believe that we can only be born here on Earth if we have contracts to fulfill in order to better the existence of those around us. When we talk with the angel council, we must inform them about what we hope to accomplish. Then, in turn, the angels will tell us about the important people and events that will Intertwine with our life to help us reach the point of remembrance so we can fulfill the contracts we have made pre-carnation.

The part that most of us forget is that we *have* made these agreements with the angels pre-carnation. During our meeting with the angel council, we will be able to see our entire lifetime laid out like a script. We'll look at events, both good and bad, that will take place in our lifetime and understand how they will benefit us, as well as shape and create the world and the people around us. At this point of being a human, we will not feel the actual pain and joy of the events that will come to pass in the future—like the tremendous grief of losing a loved one or the joy of being awarded a coveted prize. We'll see only that this grief will bring us closer to understanding our spiritual path or the difference that our hard work will make in changing the world. It is at this point that we will agree with what will come to pass, and move forward to our birth and the adventures that our life will hold.

Through this agreement with the angels, our soul is reborn into a body and positioned on this globe in the environment that will best serve the lessons or contracts we need to complete. However, because of the gift of free will, we might choose to make certain decisions that will contradict the original contracts we have made. Here on Earth, we are given many contradictory gifts that we will have to learn how to use and come out on the Other Side with grace. Free will is one such gift that comes to mind and another is the gift of ecstatic sensations. These two gifts will lead to many diverse emotions and scenarios—greed and love and all of the emotions that spin from them. On this pendulum are both the seven deadly sins and the most glorious forms of love.

And so, this is how our patterns start to emerge. Have you ever noticed that we continually make the same choices that lead down a dead-end road? Such patterns can be in areas of our life like intimate relationships, occupational choices, or communication styles. These are crossroads where we can look at ourselves honestly and possibly then realize why we are making the choices we do and how we might choose better for our soul's growth. It is within this lifetime—our sole journey here—that we will be able to open up and understand our soul's journey and why we are born into this body and this family, as well as why things happen to us as they do.

When grief causes great pain and anger to rise up inside of us, many of our positive virtues are overshadowed by the heartbreak and suffering. In this misery, we are always searching for peace of mind. Over time, as we work to diminish the hold that these emotions have on us, we begin to look within and let go of the old ideas that brought us a false sense of security. At this point, we are able to surrender, and it is in the surrendering or "giving in" that we can finally heal. When we believe there is a Higher Power, a bigger picture, a plan for all of us—and we can trust that—greater understanding and hope will begin to emerge. As we take these positive and healthy steps, we nourish and honor our soul.

Grief and loss often prompt the need to search deeper within our soul. Great sorrow can awaken us and force us to think about what it is we're supposed to be learning from this experience and where we need to go from here. The choices about our purpose in life are already there. *We* are the only ones who can change our behavior, and these actions can be very powerful. But, discovering what the choices are, especially after the death of a loved one, can be extremely challenging. Understanding that these challenges will be valuable lessons for our soul's journey will allow us to face them with more clarity and greater motivation. After all, it's about us, for us.

The word "narcissism" often has a negative

connotation, but narcissism plays a part in our sole/soul journey. How can this be? Well, ego is an important part of our humanness (the sole journey). Grief and difficult times in life often make us egocentric as we think, "this is all about my pain, my loved one, my loss, and what did I do wrong?" Our thoughts are "me, me, me," because we feel so powerless and have no control over the situation. We feel like shouting, "I could have done more. I should not have let him drive the car, go to Colorado, or play football! How could I have saved him?" Our ego is very evident in grief but, if you can bring your power back and feel even a little control, it can open the door to more control.

Spiritual narcissism is our soul journey. It occurs when we are taking care of ourselves for our spiritual growth to teach us the lessons we need to learn to fulfill our contract, to become who we are. We must begin to focus on ourselves in order to do that. In grief, we often lose focus on who we are and what our life is about. It's important to understand that, with a healthy commitment to self, we will have more control to do the hard work of grieving. Everything is about our soul's growth!

For our soul to grow, internal work is demanded. Grieving is hard work and letting go of old values and beliefs that have been carried for years is just a part of this work. Learning to trust again in a whole new way is also part of this work and part of creating a "new normal." To accomplish this, many grievers do a complete personal inventory. This encompasses a true and honest inventory on every emotion and coping skill. Sounds scary, doesn't it? Actually, as tough as it is to do, the inventory is truly helpful. It helps us discover much of what has been done in the past that was either unhealthy for us or those around us. It also is powerful to point out any actions that may be keeping us from being the person we want to be. Once we are able to identify the emotions and coping mechanisms that are unhealthy, then every one of them has to go! Again, this is not easy, but it is necessary in order to get to who we really are on a soul level, not who we think we are. Many people are confused in life by the "who we think we are" axiom where our egotistical thoughts are allowed to dominate. It's amazing what happens when we are able to clear out the old, useless "stuff" in our head. We will find that we have extra room for the goodness, growth, and enlightenment that will allow our soul to grow.

Sara believes that she was nudged to go in a new direction. One day when she had a terrible headache, she decided to take a meditative walk, searching for relief. By now, her headaches were a physical sign that she was working through something for her soul that needed to be addressed. With the pain in her head demanding relief, Sara asked Scott, "Please, let me know what I need to work on." She wasn't sure what kind of answer she would get, if any, since she felt fairly new to this type of communication.

But, as Sara exclaimed, "Suddenly, I heard the familiar words and tune to the army song in my head (Scott often sends me messages through songs!), 'Be all that you can be.'" Wow! After chuckling to herself about the song, Sara heard intuitively, "Let go of who you *think* you are (in my limited mind) and *be who you* are on a soul level." It was an amazing and thought-provoking wake-up call for Sara. Her head and heart had once again been dealing with a dis-connect that had been creating the pain. Her headache went away when she realized the full meaning of what Scott had told her! As much as Sara *hated* those headaches, they taught her a lot about herself. We all need to pay attention to what our bodies are telling us. A physician and a prescription can't fix what our soul needs. It's up to us.

It's important to remember to think with our heart, rather than so much with our often impulsive mind. Kindness, compassion, unconditional love, and forgiveness for ourselves and others will come more and more from within. Less ego-based thoughts will allow the goodness and love within our heart to flourish and be present. It's a S-O-U-L thing . . . that spiritual narcissism.

As we continue to work on our soul's growth, we may come to realize that, after many years of feeling whatever our feelings have been (perhaps anger for the misunderstanding of others), we truly can understand the words, "Be kind, be kind, for everyone is fighting some kind of battle." How is it possible that anyone can understand the enormity of our grief? If someone has not had the exact experience as we have had with our loss, how could they possibly have done everything right or said everything right in our eyes? Learning to let go of all the anger that lives within us can allow positive changes to come. It will feel as if a ten-pound weight has been lifted from our shoulders. Now, with clearer eyes and a lighter heart, it will feel *good* to look at others through kinder, more loving, more forgiving eyes. There will be a new calmness in us which is a wonderful by-product of letting go and having the opportunity to nurture our soul.

People who do this hard work will learn that honoring their soul is so important. The "who we really are" will emerge within us. We will learn to look for what feels right for us and pursue only those things. We will begin to see new beauty in ourselves, in others, and in life. We will experience greater peace and joy. Yes, JOY! And, most importantly, we will begin to feel whole again.

This work will need to be done s-o-l-e-ly, (by yourself) to get to your s-o-u-l. As Deneene told Sara, "You can't pay someone to do this work, but the benefits are priceless. They help to equalize the loss."

There is another benefit of doing this work— it will bring us even closer with our deceased loved one. It will help us look at our loved one's soul journey and understand the importance and power in it. Jane, Sara, and Deneene believe these benefits will inspire you to work hard to understand how you can remain connected to your loved one on a soul level. While doing this soul work, many people form a new relationship with God and learn that his unconditional love for them is unlimited. This brings them a new sense of peace.

We encourage you to let your heart lead you. Your heart knows who you are and where you need to be going. Trust that every experience in your life, good or bad, is an opportunity for your soul's growth. That includes the death experience. There are gifts in all of this. Of course, most of us do not want to acknowledge such a thing, and most of us don't get it for a long time. But, in time, you will see there are valuable soul lessons that can be learned through death and grief, if you are willing to accept them. Many grieving people with whom we have worked are now living rich spiritual lives and are grateful for an understanding of the meaning and power of this difficult experience. Everything is for our soul's growth.

6

Using Your Spirituality During Chaotic Times

How do you define "worldwide chaos"? Many say that worldwide chaos consists of tragedies that affect the planet. More specifically, they add that it involves disasters which have worldwide consequences. Examples of these catastrophes are terrorists' strikes that already have changed the way we travel and conduct business, nuclear explosions that could change our air quality and challenge our ability to survive their residual effects, or perhaps a devastating earthquake that could send shock waves into major population centers and kill many thousands of people.

What, then, is "private chaos"? This type of chaos is categorized as whatever upheaval happens in your life that causes you to feel disordered and confused. Examples of this are the death of a loved one, losing your home in a fire, the death of a beloved pet, or being the victim of a violent crime. As you may have probably noticed, the types of chaos that we are talking about are all initiated by external causes, meaning that the act is done to you or the hurt comes from something that is outside of your body.

But, there also is an "internal chaos," which is a severe depression or anxiety that keeps your mind racing or feeling disjointed. It can be a self-induced confusion about determining the best way to complete a task or begin a new one. It even can be self-doubt or poor self-esteem that causes you to wonder how your thoughts are being created. Yet another type of internal chaos, which will be discussed in this chapter, comes through physical illness and pain. Learning how your spiritual beliefs create these states of total confusion and illness will help you gain more control over them.

Because this book is about loss, the remainder of this chapter will be dedicated to how chaos complicates grief and blocks spirituality. Jane recently asked her client, Annie, what her grief would be like if she felt confident that her deceased son could hear her and she could hear him. What would it be like if she felt sure that he is with her, and the only difference from when he was on a physical plane is that he no longer is in pain and she can't give him a hug or physically see his face? Annie replied that her grief would be totally different and she believed it would be less intense. The next question was, "Why not adopt this belief structure, and work toward being open to your son's communications?"

This helped Annie make the decision to take the steps necessary to be able to listen and to learn from her son.

Jane began working with grieving people more than twenty years ago. She learned that there was no clear grief therapy that had high rates of success. She also found that the clients who had the most severe and debilitating grief reactions were parents who had lost a child. So, Jane researched therapies that had been most helpful for the parents of a child who had died suddenly at an age between fourteen and twenty-eight. After talking with many parents, she determined that the primary helpful factor was having a continuing relationship with their deceased child. Of course, most of these parents had different definitions for this continuing relationship and each also applied it uniquely. Some connected through past memories. Others connected spiritually. Still others felt connected through living family members who also remembered the deceased child. In the years since Jane's study was completed, she has used the information she learned from it in her private grief counseling practice to help parents gain a sense of control over their grief, become functional in their home and work lives, and keep their deceased loved one in their hearts, minds, and souls. By an overwhelming percentage, those clients who have created a spiritual loving connection have gained the most grief relief and function in their lives. Of course, this evidence is anecdotal, but compelling enough that Jane has dedicated her professional life to spreading the word so that many others can be helped in similar ways.

As you may have already learned, your grief and your spirituality are both unique to you. They are dependent on what you create and develop. This power to create forms the foundation of experience and knowledge that you can lean into during chaotic times in your life. If this foundation is not already in place in your life, it will take some time and energy to determine your beliefs and comfort zone. However, this time and effort will be well worth it! This book will help you make these decisions about your wants, needs, and abilities to live a spiritual life.

All experiences that we have here on Earth are about our soul's growth. Everything that we do creates a lesson for our soul. Living on Earth means that we will be entirely and perfectly egocentric. Nothing that we do in this lifetime goes unnoticed. However, it is our soul that does the noticing, and determines if the deeds will be processed in a positive or negative way. Many people believe that God makes these decisions. Others believe that the karma earned in past lifetimes will create life experiences during this lifetime. Whatever your belief system may be, it is a good one because it is yours and you own it.

Many of you may have experienced unhelpful comments by other people during your loved one's calling hours. You may or may not remember each comment, but we guarantee that the person who said it remembers it, is embarrassed by it, and possibly even feels shamed. The comment marked that person's soul, not yours. Each and every time the person thinks of it, shame is felt. Can you forgive that person? Will your forgiveness make a difference in that person? Maybe, or maybe not. Their comment was not about you and your soul's work. It was about their soul and their soul's work.

Jane's older daughter, Stephanie, attended Saint Mary's College in Notre Dame, Indiana. While there, Stephanie was required to take a religion class. She told Jane that her professor challenged every belief that she and her classmates had. She learned that it was not the teachings of the church that were important, but that the students learned what they believed and, more importantly, why they believed. This is the very same task that we are asking you to do. Leaning into a belief system that possibly was learned by rote will not help you during chaotic times. Knowing why you believe what you believe is imperative and life saving when you face both external and internal chaos.

External Chaos
Using Your Spirituality During Worldwide Chaos

How did the September 11, 2001, terror

attacks on the United States affect you? Were you filled with fear, anger, anxiety, and sadness? Did you rail at God, the attackers, and the world? September 11 had many different affects. Some children believed we were being attacked over and over again because of the television coverage constantly showing the planes going into the Twin Towers and into the Pentagon. Fortunately, there was no visual of the plane going into the ground in Pennsylvania. Many children were frightened and had trouble sleeping, returning to school, and functioning in their day-to-day lives. Did your reaction match the children's?

Generally, adults also found it difficult to talk about anything but the attacks. The productivity of American companies during the week following the attacks was reportedly at its lowest since Black Monday when the stock market crashed. Of course, we understand the necessity to talk about this tragedy. We were all trying to "make sense out of nonsense." How could this tragedy happen on American soil? We just couldn't believe it, nor did our minds and hearts want to believe it. How could we assimilate the loss of so many of our fellow Americans? Having a spiritual belief system allows people to come to some understanding of this kind of global incident. Many believe everything that happens provides an opportunity to learn. Of course, we'd certainly rather not learn in this way, but some think these lessons are the reason for our human existence. Others believe that mass departures are planned for souls who are unable to complete their work under current world societies. Others think that bad things happen to good people and there is no true answer as to why these things happen. No matter what belief structure you have about the horrors that occur, it is important for you to lean into your beliefs to become as functional and understanding of others as you can be. It is important, as spiritual beings, to understand that everyone has the right to their own beliefs. We might not agree or even like their beliefs, but it is not up to us to judge. Our responsibility is to be loving and caring. This can be a true test of our spirituality!

Using Your Spirituality During Personal Chaos

Our assumption is that, if you are reading this book, you have experienced personal chaos through the death of a loved one. This kind of chaos is experienced through the feelings of disbelief, shock, horror, sometimes anger, and always sadness. It is the kind of chaos that shakes you to your very core. It matters not that you thought you had been prepared for the death. Hospice workers are dear sweet souls who often remark that, even though a deceased loved one had been in a hospice program for months, their family is shocked when the death occurs. They remark that the common battle cry of those families is, "I wasn't ready" or "I didn't think she would die so soon."

Some of us think we are prepared and almost feel relieved after the suffering has ended. However, it is still an assault and shock to our system when we pick up the phone expecting to hear the voice of our loved one, only to find it is a hospice worker calling to say that death has come. This reaction is normal and a part of our grief process, but it triggers the chaotic lifestyle of grief.

As for most people, it's so important to know what you believe about where your loved one is. Many find their connections begin when they are able to place their loved one in heaven, on the Other Side, or at the next place. This is the first step in forming that loving connection. We believe that, if it's helpful to see your loved one somewhere, you should do so in as much detail as you can. Be as specific as possible. Visualize what your loved one is wearing and doing, and what the surroundings are like. Also, begin visualizing others who are with your loved one and what their relationships are like as well as what you want your loved one's relationship to be with you. This is a foundational piece to using your spirituality during personal chaos and, when practiced and assimilated into your life, it will serve you well.

Internal Chaos
Depression, Anxiety, Fear

Internal chaos is the turmoil that comes from inside our body. Sometimes this is caused by a brain chemistry that isn't in balance. Sometimes it stems from living a lifestyle that is stressful and unhealthy. Other times, this confusion comes from hereditary factors. It doesn't really matter how it comes to you. What you *do* about working through it is most important.

When your internal chaos stems from hereditary factors or imbalanced brain chemistry, it is important that you seek and gain medical help. We are so fortunate to be living in a time when there are wonderful medications that can assist our brains to function properly. Please consult your physician if you are plagued by depression that does not allow you to function, comes and goes or comes at specific times of the year, or if you have anxiety that prevents you from living an independent and full life. Be honest with the physician about your sleeping and eating patterns as well as about how you are functioning throughout the day and night. Hopefully, you will also consult a counselor who can help you live with this imbalance, adjust to the medication, and problem solve ways to lead a full life. Oftentimes, counselors are able to spot problems before they become full blown so that you can deal with the problems before they cause too much chaos in your life.

One of Jane's clients, Emma, told her that fear is really the acronym "f.e.a.r." meaning "*f*alse *e*motions *a*ppearing *r*eal." Emma was grieving the loss of her daughter and the fears that she faced during that time proved to be mostly false. For example, she was terribly afraid she would not be able to live through the first anniversary of her daughter, Susan's, murder. She was truly physically ill for weeks before. She was sure that others would not remember her Susan on this terrible day. She also believed that no one would understand her need to stay in her home and be alone. She thought that she would be fired from her job for taking this day off because a big meeting had been scheduled. She thought her heart would break, all over again, knowing that she hadn't seen Susan's beautiful brown eyes in 365 days. None of these fears was realized. She did live through the tragic anniversary and did not lose her job. Of course, her heart felt as if it was breaking all over again, but somehow it continued to beat in her chest, bringing life-giving blood to her organs.

Emma has now been able to lean into a continuing relationship with Susan. It has provided her a way to feel Susan's love and commitment in times of internal chaos. Emma is living her life for herself, for both of her daughters (surviving and deceased), and for the people in the grief group that she co-facilitates. She has been able to help the group members recognize the "f.e.a.r." and head these emotions off at the pass!

Physical Illness and Pain

Just like with grief, physical illness is a difficult time to learn to lead a spiritual life. However, it sometimes just happens that way.

In 1983, Jane was diagnosed with breast cancer. She was very ill and needed all of her inner power to go through the three separate surgeries—a lumpectomy, mastectomy, and hysterectomy—that would occur within four weeks' time. At the conclusion of these surgeries, Jane endured seven months of chemotherapy that made her physically sick more days than not and robbed her of the strength she needed to perform her teaching responsibilities and, more importantly, care for her two daughters who were then seven and two years of age.

Jane was born and raised in the Methodist Church. She had a strong belief in God but, for several years, had been working toward a spiritual life that brought in more possibilities than those taught through any one organized religion. She hadn't really put these possibilities into play in her own life in any dedicated way, but continued to read and ponder the potential during the time of her illness.

In the 1980s, the anti-nausea drugs were not as helpful as they can be today. This meant that, for several days each week, Jane was challenged to find ways to get through the crippling nausea. She knew either she could succumb to it or she could work to get her mind on something else. Reading, watching television, playing games, and sewing all provided no relief. Jane had been given several books by Dr. Bernie

Siegel and decided to use meditation to work with, instead of against, the chemo. She had not been schooled in meditation nor had she ever practiced it with success or regularity. However, she now began to use prayer as the foundational piece of her meditation. During the months of chemo, Jane actually became quite good at meditation and found that it gave her some peace from the physical ills as well as the mental anguish of possibly not being able to see her daughters grow up.

Sara, Deneene, and Jane have all experienced personal struggles of their own that brought them to this juncture. Thus, they speak from true understanding and a love for their fellow man and woman. They recognize that, whether a loss is from the death of a loved one, personal illness, or ongoing struggles of life, being committed to living a spiritual life and appreciating that the bonds of love are not broken add up to a wonderful way to live.

Summary

We all understand the difficult and seemingly impossible feat of controlling our minds and bodies to do this work. Once proficient, harnessing your spirituality will allow your body and mind to work for you. You will learn to know your soul and how you are related to this universe and the next place. Chaos happens! Whether internal, external, or spiritual, the crises that are inherent in this lifetime will continue. Learning how to identify these crises and prepare ourselves to adjust to them has been the focus of this chapter.

Think of examples in your own life when you have known that you were one with your Creator, your Higher Power, and your soul. Under what other circumstances would it be helpful to feel that connection, to truly know that each and every experience is about your soul's growth, and to understand that your loved one is just a blink of an eye away?

Think of the times when you are driving and your car is behind a driver who doesn't go through the traffic light the moment that it turns green or a driver who is (heaven forbid!) driving UNDER the speed limit. Do you ever think, "That person might have saved me from a speeding ticket or from an accident"? Do you realize that we are all connected and the act of someone else can present a way for us to grow?

Leading a spiritual life that will help you in chaotic times takes daily work and a warrior-like personality. It requires you to build a strong spirit that you will feel confident to rely on. It takes dedication and practice so that when you need to lean into this spirituality (and when *don't* we?), it will be there—ready and waiting.

7

What's Stopping You from Living the Spiritual Life You Want and Deserve?

When we ask people what is stopping them from living the spiritual life they want and deserve, many of the same reasons keep coming up. Such as; fear, guilt, shame, taking the responsibility and being accountable for living a spiritual life and the time, effort and discipline this entails, what others may say, etc. Some of us are already trudging a spiritual journey and are very aware of what we want our spiritual life to look like. Others don't know how to even begin their travels. In this chapter, we explore some of the essential roadblocks to living amidst the spirit, and then help you to lay out your own spiritual map. You will probably find that, as you move through the different levels of becoming acquainted with your spiritual journey, the more you will become naturally attuned to it.

The first step in beginning your spiritual journey is to define what it is not or, rather, to identify and seek to avoid those roadblocks that probably affect all of us at one time or another.

- I don't know where to start. How do I go about being more spiritual?
- I fear that those I love will abandon me or not need me anymore.
- I don't have enough time to dedicate to my spiritual journey because of my fast-paced lifestyle.
- I have nowhere or no one to go to where I can feel safe exploring new ideas.
- I fear the unknown of where this path will lead me.
- I think it is selfish for me to take time for my spiritual journey when others in my life are in need.
- I fear that my spiritual journey will leave me with economic insecurity.

These are just a few of the entrenched patterns that halt our thought processes. Each person has their own unique patterns. In order to honor your spiritual journey, take a moment right now to write down the reasons that you believe are stopping you from living the spiritual life you want and deserve. After that, write down what your spiritual life would look like if there was nothing or no one standing in your way.

It is very understandable that the roadblocks mentioned above, or those that are unique to you, have prevented you from living the spiritual life you want and deserve. However, if you truly want a spiritual life, it will take a feverish dedication and commitment. The first step is having faith and believing in a Higher Power, whatever that Higher Power is to you. You then need to set a goal for yourself and take small steps toward it. They need to be small, manageable steps—ones that you can accomplish without having to tackle the entire large piece. The large piece is always attained just a little at a time. When it is finally achieved, you will look back and find that altogether you have paved the path for your own fulfillment—one breath, one step, one moment at a time.

Vigilance is crucial in this process. We are too accustomed to being part of a lazy society where we set lofty personal goals and then break promises to ourselves because we haven't the fortitude or the discipline to see them through.

Let's take any external crutch (for example, like overeating). You'd probably make a goal for losing 50 pounds instead of concentrating gently on walking for 20, 15, or 10 minutes a day. You can walk yourself or diet yourself until the cows come home but, if you do not acknowledge the fundamental spiritual deficiency in using the external crutch in the first place, your spiritual journey is stunted. In fact, you are embarking on a physical path without any spiritual underpinnings. Thus, we can almost guarantee that your weight will return because you have not found that fundamental spiritual connection or addressed the emptiness or fear within that has led you down a negative self-path in the first place. Conversely, imagine yourself as a much thinner person because you have set short-term, manageable goals with the intent of the long-term reward.

Spiritual and physical cohesion are attainable, but a voracious desire and a willingness to follow through are nonnegotiable along that journey. In fact, if you are at an all-time low today, if you are so sad and lost that you feel there is nothing that could ever make you whole again, then you are luckier than someone who has not yet reached that point. For that is the human condition that many of us have to face BEFORE we can be willing to try anything to feel whole again. This may be your Higher Power's way of leading you toward the light, not away from it. So, give yourself permission to rejoice in your misery because a new day can dawn this very minute.

Now, let's say that you are in touch with the spiritual piece, but not as comfortable with the action piece (and remember both are essentials, one cannot stand in the midst of energy and hope to obtain a PhD through osmosis). It is so important that we keep the promises we make to ourselves, to our souls. As we said before, you'll be discouraged in a week or two if you want lose those 50 pounds immediately. However, in that same two weeks, you could have walked every day to lift your self-esteem so high that you had the courage to add another 10 minutes to your walk. From there, you'll have found the self-love to join a group of overeaters, read a nutrition book, and educate yourself to make healthier eating choices. This commitment to our soul once we have set a goal is key to keeping our minds, hearts, and souls in sync (see Chapter 9 about the power to create). When we make resolutions to change but do not follow through, we do damage to our soul. Our soul stops taking us seriously. Let us repeat: OUR SOUL STOPS TAKING US SERIOUSLY. If we could tell you anything, it would be to stop making promises to yourself that you cannot or will not keep. That is why we emphasize baby steps, tangible steps, that we can almost touch.

It can seem overwhelming to someone who is grieving or in great pain to even begin to contemplate finding the spiritual life they desire. It may feel like it will take too much work, take too much time, and perhaps even be too much to even think about. Like in so many other challenges, if we have some good guidelines or suggestions, we can begin to take one step at a time until we feel more comfortable and knowledgeable about the direction in which we are going. As our confidence builds, we will see ourselves achieving more than we ever could have imagined. We just have to start. Below, we've listed some "how-tos" that may be helpful in guiding you to that spiritual life you want and deserve.

Choose One *Small* Thing and Commit to It

Don't get overwhelmed by adding something new and big to your life. Begin with something small and manageable, but meaningful. Commit to that. Promise yourself that you are going to do this one thing every day because you know it will be good for you. Also, a wonderful spiritual exercise is being grateful. Start by writing three reasons why you are grateful each day and you'll see that life offers much goodness to you, even in small doses.

Stop Playing It Safe

You've probably heard some version of the saying, "You will either move forward into growth or you will fall back into safety." What will you do? Playing it safe offers no growth and limits the possibilities for the new spiritual life you want. Are you willing to expand your horizons and create a new and meaningful life for yourself? Don't limit yourself on this journey. Discover new things about life and yourself!

Understand the Soul's Journey on a Human Level

Armed with the knowledge that your soul's growth is WHY you are here on this earth plane, you can focus on your soul's journey with more discretion and fervor. On a human level, we make choices daily that will take us in either a positive or a negative direction. With every thought we make and every action we take every single day, we have control over those choices. By valuing yourself, and making wise and healthy decisions, you will nourish your soul's journey.

Stop Resisting Change

In our grief and pain, we often resist change and avoid moving in new directions. You may be scared of letting go and don't trust that life can be meaningful once again. But, eventually, we all learn that life moves us on whether or not we want to move. We are constantly offered new opportunities to change and grow. If you can embrace change, rather than resist it, you will find that new doors open to offer wonderful experiences and people who can enrich your life, leading you to the spiritual life you want and desire.

Stop Thinking "I Don't Deserve to Be Happy" or "I Don't Want to Be Happy"

Everyone goes through some type of difficult or debilitating situation in their life. Unfortunately, grief and loss, divorce, depression, and other life-changing events can create feelings of not wanting to be happy or that we are undeserving of happiness. Self-worth and self-love suffer. At these times, we must remember that, spiritually, we are all meant to be happy in life. If we limit ourselves by not allowing that happiness, we will not be able to live a rich spiritual life. So, look for ways to love yourself and to cherish the gifts you have been blessed with. Happiness will come from within, when you look within.

Find a Halfway Point Between Desires and Commitments

Look at your schedule each day and find a way to fit your spiritual goal into your life in the best way that you can. Whatever task you've determined to achieve on your spiritual journey, there will be a means to achieve it. You may have to get up early, stay up late, or work on it during your lunch break. You will discover a way that works best for you.

Be Satisfied

Be satisfied with what you CAN do. It is a huge success to do even ONE thing differently for one minute of your day. Be happy you've given yourself that minute, that time. Don't minimize it.

Make Promises

Making promises to yourself and to your spirit is important to your soul's growth. When you say "I promise," the energy will come to help you. If you hold these promises so that your soul understands you are serious and committed, it will help create the time needed to turn these commitments into reality.

Develop a Warrior-Type Personality

You need to have a warrior-type personality when you dedicate yourself to change. This is work you do by yourself, for yourself. Value yourself and your soul enough to act. Sitting back and waiting for it to happen will not bring the desired results you want. Just do it!

Let Your Thoughts Create

Everything we think about creates an action. Have you ever had someone tell you that you look ill in the morning and, by midafternoon, you feel sick? The simple response of, "Do I?" to that person's question has the power to allow sickness to enter your body. Responding with, "No, I feel fine!" will instead send that message to your body and you *will* feel great.

Create Constantly

Just as your thoughts create, so do your words and actions. Being positive about yourself, your family, friends, pets, and the world at large will create positive energies to be focused on all those areas. We *do* have the power to change ourselves and the world.

Forge Ahead So the Soul Can Grow

As humans, we have a job to do. We choose to come to Earth to have the experiences we need to learn and grow. Everything that we experience is "soul growing." It doesn't matter if you see it that way or not. It is all about growing your soul. Your experiences will go into unlearning fear, ego, greed, and judgments. They will also allow you to learn kindness, love, and spiritual wisdom.

Use Positive Affirmations

Affirmations are a simple way to start yourself on a successful spiritual journey. By using positive, self-affirming words each day, we encourage positive thinking. We know that thoughts create so, by repeating these positive words, we begin to take responsibility for what we think and say. Write several positive personal statements. Make a commitment to speak these meaningful affirmations for thirty days, and you will be showing the universe your desire to become the best you can be. Affirmations encourage self-love and acceptance, and your reward will be seeing the spiritual life you want and deserve begin to evolve.

Summary

What's stopping you from living the life you want and deserve? Is it money, fear, health, time, shame, guilt, grief, depression, thoughts of others, obligations, religious teachings, marriages, moral and ethical teachings? Think about this. Take some time to write your personal reasons for not feeling healthy or satisfied with your present life due to your grief. Determining what the grief issues are and acknowledging them can help you start on a path to greater spiritual peace, happiness, and fulfillment.

8

Making the Commitment to Survive
and
Believing in Life Again

Grief, pain, guilt, suffering, anguish. . . . at some point in our life, whether we want to think about it or not, we will have to find our way through a major loss and the heartache that accompanies it. There's no way around it. We can fight, ignore, or reject the inevitable trauma of death and loss, but we won't win this battle. It's a grueling task to deal with grief. The limited energy available to us during the grieving process typically runs out, and we end up feeling empty. We begin to suffer with it physically, mentally, and emotionally, and we feel desperate and unprepared. That is when we have to acknowledge that some type of change must occur within.

In this chapter, we will explore the reality of grief and the need to make a commitment to survive when our life takes such an unexpected and unwanted turn. Once we gain a greater understanding of how we react to devastating, life-altering circumstances, we will be able to see with more clarity and in time believe that life is again worth living. It's all a part of the grief journey, and there's much to learn along the way.

When we suffer the death of someone we love, or face a major loss, we must embrace the heartache. Grief is the emotional roller coaster we experience that takes us places we've never known or seen before. Often the grief is created suddenly. No matter how we receive the shocking news—via a phone call, person to person, or in some other way—our life will never again be the same. Deep, agonizing reactions typically follow after hearing the news, with anguish, fear, shock, anger, despair, and helplessness being only a few of the emotions that create the horror that ensues. Often life itself is questioned. Most of us even question our will to live. We don't have an active death wish, but we do have a passive life wish. This means that we aren't planning our own death, but we don't care if it comes. It means that we are ready to go to heaven and be with our loved one again.

Initially, we need to deal with the immensity of the grief. The tears must come and we must feel the pain. It is healthy for these emotions to flow out of us. Keeping them in causes "dis-ease" and we don't need to complicate our grief with physical illness. We somehow have to begin living a life without our loved one being physically in it. Every single day is challenging for us as we face the reality and enormity of our loss. Some of us will retreat into what appears to be a dark tunnel. This place feels safe, far away from society and the daily life that continues to go on with the rest of the world. In the tunnel, we cry long and hard, and feel the depth of our pain without interference from well-meaning "helpful Hannahs" telling us to move on, get over it, and put on a happy face. But, how can we do that when we consider that we're honoring our loved one by grieving so deeply? Feeling like a victim comes more easily and there is no one in the tunnel to tell us otherwise. It feels so safe to avoid the outside world. But, is staying in the tunnel healthy? No one can determine how long anyone should grieve. . . We're all so different, but isolating ourselves can create a host of other problems. We are often so overwhelmed by the enormity of the loss that we cannot see life through clear eyes. It takes time to absorb the reality of the death of someone we love so much, and we can't pretend it doesn't hurt. During this time, we must make many choices. Some are good for us, some not so good. Some make sense, and some don't. In the end, we are simply trying to find our way out of the dark, and to somehow survive.

So, how do we even make a commitment to survive? Do we just suddenly ask if we truly want to survive this terrible loss? After the grieving period has been well established, and for many, has become long lasting, most of us will admit that we were never able to say we wanted to survive. It is a long slow process of taking one step at a time but, perhaps unconsciously, we are making steps to survive. This is sometimes done in ways where we find some relief. It might be going to counseling, journaling, meditating, going to church, attending a support group, or reading about the work of grief.

Counseling is the method many of us will choose. Quality time one-on-one with a counselor who understands overwhelming grief can be tremendously helpful and healthy. Tears can flow, questions about grief can be answered or discussed, and we can be gently guided toward healing.

Attending a support group is another positive step that may be taken. Sharing with others who understand our grief and loss can be therapeutic, helpful, and bring much-needed relief from feelings of isolation. Along with the positive aspects of support, often new feelings of friendship and compassion for others in the group arise. We begin to think about others and their pain. The incredible pain is now shared and thoughts of surviving may not be so overwhelming.

In time, because life will try to push us on, we need to find a new normal. This is a difficult concept to understand and many balk at the possibility. We don't believe that life will ever be normal again, but we are missing the word "new." We will fight this until we finally realize there really is no choice but to establish new everyday norms. We cannot stay in our old normal; it doesn't exist any longer. That's a very hard truth to accept. But, we need to begin to understand and believe that we can bring our loved one into our life in other ways and, in doing that, we'll keep them close. We can talk to them, memorialize them in beautiful and meaningful ways, fix their favorite foods, and share who they were with others. We have to allow ourselves to find that new normal, and eventually we will realize it is a much healthier place to be in—mentally, physically, and spiritually. Thankfully, the result of this effort is that, in time, we will find relief in this new place.

The death of someone we love often opens our minds and hearts to new and unexpected happenings that can encourage a renewed interest in life. Most of us find much peace when we open our minds to the signs that our loved one is sending. Of course, this necessitates a knowledge that our loved one exists. Many of us work hard so that our loved one will be proud of us. This is a huge motivator for us to embrace the pain and find ways to create and accept this new normal. This will lead most of us toward giving ourselves permission to live with the pain instead of continuing to struggle so fiercely against it. The suffering that had long reminded us of the death becomes a gentler reminder of the great love we felt for our loved one. Making a promise to our loved one to never give up, to create a new normal, and to find peace is both a wonderful and attainable goal.

These steps certainly are not easy and, unfortunately, we can't make them any less difficult for you. Grief is often thought to be more powerful and stronger than we are. But, this is not true. We must take each experience and situation day by day, or even hour by hour. We'll find that there still will be bad days, but the opportunity increases for better days when we face the grief and do the hard work that follows. Many spiritual lessons are being learned with every positive step we take. We try to remember, as we push ourselves a little farther with each step, that we are the only ones who can do this crucial work.

In the quest for greater understanding, peace, and connections with our loved ones, we find that we begin to unburden ourselves of many emotions that have plagued us and held us hostage, often for years. This encourages us to make a stronger commitment to life and living. An important and necessary step that we must take is to release the built-up fear and anger we have carried for so long. By doing this work, we open up the opportunity to forgive others, which is so necessary for our well-being. The negativity we feel in grief is overwhelming, and often all consuming. We blame others because we are hurt so much by their words or actions that we get stuck and can go forward with no positive momentum. Releasing these emotions and forgiving others, even many years later, can bring us added relief—mentally, physically, and spiritually.

Grief infiltrates nearly every aspect of our life, and we are usually unaware of how many ways this can happen. Making a firm commitment to life, or even an unconscious one, requires that we need to assimilate the loss into our daily life. This often takes us out of our comfort zone, typically because we avoid the toughest issues in grief. This may be a result of our lack of energy or desire, our anger, or again our fear. By avoiding these issues, they become even bigger hurdles to developing our new normal, and can interrupt the connections we so desire with our loved one. Assimilating the death into every aspect of our life opens up blocks that were created in grief. Our loved one wants to be a part of our life and hopes that, by working through the grief, we may be able to connect in a whole new way. We will begin to open ourselves up to new, and even wondrous, things in our life.

We have to decide whether or not we want to survive these traumatic and life-changing events. Our individual reasons to survive are often overshadowed by pain, anger, and other powerful emotions. If we keep in touch with, and appreciate our reasons to go on, we'll recognize that our life has great meaning and value. We all have reasons for surviving, but we have to acknowledge and embrace those reasons. Families may be a big reason to go on living, as we find we need each other's support during these difficult times. Loving friends and pets also give us reasons to survive. Our jobs and volunteering can be meaningful sources of fulfillment. Our loved one on the Other Side will recognize our value in this life and understand we are here because we are supposed to be and we have a need to continue fulfilling our contracts. We are still here for a reason. Believe that! We need to see our strengths, not our weaknesses, because we are stronger than we think we are . . . even after grief has entered our life. There's an inner strength in all of us that, when given the opportunity, will emerge . . . if we don't stuff it back down. Search for your strength, use it, and value it.

We may find that our purpose in life becomes clearer as we release old pain and search for new meaning. Sometimes we might find it fulfilling to facilitate or co-facilitate a support group for others. Helping others in their painful journey with the experiences and knowledge gained through our own grief can be rewarding. This can also be a confidence booster and help with reinvestment in our life. Often we will find ways to use our experiences by volunteering in organizations where we can reach out to others in memory of our loved one. This can be extremely satisfying work. For example, Lifebanc is a healing place for Marti who lovingly donated her son, Matthew's organs as she helps educate the community on the need for organ donation. Jim whose wife, Linda, was killed by a drunk driver volunteers many heartfelt hours to MADD. Andy whose son, Christopher, was murdered sponsors a blood drive in Christopher's name. Reinvesting in life is a part of the grief process that enables us to live with the loss as well as contribute toward making the world a better place. Often this heartfelt work is done in our loved one's memory and the commitment to life becomes stronger through such loving actions. We discover that we can do things we never imagined possible, and that is surprisingly satisfying as we move through our grief.

As we continue to lift the weight of grief off our shoulders, we also must actively search for peace from the chaos that has filled our life. Many of us may feel that we will never find peace following the death of our loved one, but by working diligently to let go of the many obstacles to that elusive sense of peace, we ultimately will discover a new spirituality. This will bring insights about life and death that most of us never knew existed. Seeing a greater picture of why we are here on the earth plane allows us to make great strides in our healing. It's helpful to understand and believe that our loved one's death was not a random act by God, or anyone else, but that there is a plan for each of us in this lifetime, designed by us in our individual pre-birth contracts. For many, this new information is comforting and, as the understanding increases, so does the comfort. We will know that our loved one still exists, quite happily on the Other Side, and is patiently waiting for us to emerge from the stronghold of grief. It's also important to understand that our loved one does not judge our grief response. Our loved one knows that every emotion and behavior we experience is about our soul's growth. Truly, every occurrence is useful as we embark on the life we will live before, during, and after our loss.

It is so difficult to believe in life again. However, if we look hard enough, we will see that there is another side to grief. It will show itself when we actually allow ourselves to view life on the opposite side of the pain and suffering. Our broken heart demands a greater understanding of death, and of how the amazing signs and messages we receive from our loved one most certainly do occur. Working hard to acquire a new normal and realizing a life that has greater meaning can bring increased hope for our future. It can't stop there. We cannot let it stop there. We've traveled a long, tough grief journey, not of our choice, but most definitely a journey of substance.

Knowledge about our soul's journey may encourage us to believe in our life again. Maybe we had no prior knowledge about this journey, but now is the time to begin our search for the information to use. If we believe in our soul's journey, we know that our present life has great value and meaning. Our soul is here on this planet to learn and experience many new things. All the experiences that confront us can provide growth for our soul. Individually, we make the choices about whether or not we will try to overcome the challenges that we face. Most of us have not been familiar at all with the soul's journey before our loved one's death. As we gain information about the significance of the death to our personal journey, we will find courage to work toward healing and greater understanding. We will learn that our loved one has completed their soul journey at the age that they died, no matter how young they may have been. When we truly recognize this, it will bring us peace.

There are many unforeseen gifts that will encourage us to look at the other side of grief. Appreciation of these unexpected and beautiful gifts will enhance our life in many extraordinary ways. There may be new friends, sincerely good new friends who grace our doors or perhaps even our computer screens through chat rooms. There also may be kindnesses shown and support given from people we barely knew before our loved one died or from people we have known forever. We may be given opportunities to reach out to others with an increased compassion that comes from a grieving heart. We will always have the memories of our loved one. Memories that initially brought pain and tears will become cherished details of our loved one's life. Perhaps we will achieve a greater awareness of spirituality and how it offers not only the answers to life and death, but also that long-awaited sense of peace. We will know what is important in life because we will have grown with the grief. The list of gifts goes on and on. Each of us will have our own special collection and each gift is a reason why we can believe in life again. We will be able to see life through clearer eyes and a grateful heart, and believe in the goodness that life will continue to offer.

Every one of us can grow and be strengthened by this most difficult and challenging experience. If we honestly look at ourselves, we'll see that we have much to offer this world. We can't stop midway through the journey and live a life mired in the muck of grief. Our loss will always be a part of us, but so will our love for that special person. We will hold on to the wonderful memories and love we shared. Yet, we also have choices to make that can take us to new places in our hearts and elsewhere. Believing in life again is challenging. But, let's allow ourselves to accept this great challenge to grow and heal. Let us honor our loved one with all of our strength and courage. Let us share our gifts and experience for the betterment of the world.

Remember, "They like us, aware that it is through the enduring struggles of life that we redefine ourselves. We are bereft and we are weak, but we know what it means to be truly brave and strong." (Norman J. Fried, *The Angel Letters: Lessons That Dying Can Teach Us About Living*, Chicago: Ivan Dee, 2007, p. 43).

9

The Power to Create: A Human Experience

As grievers, feeling powerless becomes something that feels comfortable and familiar. The aim of this chapter is to give you a glimpse into the natural conjecture of "the power to create" and the ability to have more input and control over your life. Creation is a gift that has been bestowed on each of us, a talent that simply needs a little attention and nurturance, especially after being beaten down by grief and loss. When we see all the books that have come to light about the power to create, we want to create "stuff" for ourselves. We feel it is our God-given right to produce all of these "things" for our life; to envision, and thus stumble effortlessly upon wealth, health, and the like. We want to create the perfect job, the perfect companion, the perfect car and feel that the death of our loved one is not the end of our life. Of course, we understand that it is the death of the kind of life we once had, but using the power to create a new life including our loved one in a new way is very valuable. The ironic thing is that, although we can use the power to create for our own life, it is in this self-centered manifestation of our desire for power that we evade finding true satisfaction. The gift of power is not just about creating for ourselves. We have been given this process of manifestation not to enrich our pocketbooks, but to create and manifest unconditional love for humanity and our planet. It is only when we align our intentions with the right purpose that those other objectified versions of abundance simply fall into place. Our hope is to help you see the need for this "creating" on an individual, a communal and a global level.

And, as with all change, the journey begins within us.

Perception is what the power to create is all about. If we can perceive, imagine, and envision the way that we would like to be or not be, we are already on the first step toward creating "a new me." Everyone has this power, this potential. Unfortunately, we often see ourselves as victims to our circumstances and are shrouded by our experiences. However, our imagination gives us the opportunity to look at a situation with "new glasses." Do we want to be a victim to what happens to us, or to empower ourselves from the exact same situation? Life is all an illusion, an illusion that is based on our perception at any given moment. So, why not take these experiences and transcend them to their true spiritual meanings? All of our experiences can be vehicles to draw us closer to our Higher Power, to see our true meaning, and to help us find purpose for our individual life. Isn't that what we really want to know? Why have we had such traumatic losses? Why are we here? What is our existence on Planet Earth all about? What can we contribute? Not to mention, what are the "whys" of humanity?

It is when we can begin to put these pieces together, and to do so with the intent of seeking harmony so that we may offer it elsewhere, that our true contracts will emerge. It is then that we will stop feeling like a victim and transcend our perspective, illusion, or viewpoint to understanding. On the journey of bringing this purpose from Earth to heaven, and then back into our life, we manifest that experience into light airy gold. Only then can we look at our experiences differently, understand them on a much higher level, and finally be able to smile again as we regain joy and peace in our life. Especially after such significant loss.

Let us take the grief of a parent who has lost a child as an example. That is some of the heaviest lead anyone can carry in their life and in their soul. If you are reading this and have a child who has died, we are sure you are thinking that there is *no* way to ever lose this terrible feeling of loss and sorrow. Of course, this book will not relieve you of your loss. But, if you can understand why the child you have lost was in your life, why you were blessed with this wonderful relationship for what seems a fleeting amount of time, how you were able to help your child fulfill their set contract by learning what was required of their life here on

Earth, and how their life and death helped you and your family, it will grace you with new meaning and perspective about this heartbreaking experience that you can carry with you always. Now, as you trudge this difficult journey of loss, your feet will lighten, and you will see that this tragic event had a purpose and perceive its significance in a new light.

Without this perception on the prism of grief, life can become overwhelming. Breathing, let alone showering, can seem like the most daunting of tasks. How can we cease to feel imprisoned and weighed down by our experiences, discover their meaning, and embrace the lessons of these tragic events? Well, as three people who have grieved many times in our own lives, we can tell you that, while possible, it is not easy. This search for serenity in the midst of sadness is available to all, but it can be attained only by those vigilant enough to want it voraciously.

That is what applying the power to create is about. It provides the tools for perceiving our reality in a different light. It utilizes the main principal behind alchemy: to change lead into gold. Our experiences shape who we are and mold us throughout our lifetime. But, the experience of grief is heavy. It weighs us down because it is equal to lead. Consequently, we can hardly lift up our heads to make it through the day. Even when we learn to function again despite that grief, we walk around with the heaviness of it as an unwanted escort in our soul. We find it difficult to retrieve the joy that might come to us because the weight of the grief is so dense, so dark, that we cannot see the light. Although these heart-wrenching experiences are a part of our framework and make up whom we are, this book has offered you the tools to help transform the darkness into light. This transformation begins with embracing where you are right now, today.

The key ingredient in this transformation, and one of the most important tools we possess, is our *imagination*. We often don't realize the phenomenal gift that we have been given with the power of imagination. If we can think of something and imagine it, we can be it. We may not be the best of the best. We may not become Mozart if we choose to play the piano but, if we can envision ourselves behind the piano playing a tune when we have never before touched a keyboard, we will be closer to achieving what was once the unachievable. Our soul is capable of so much—we just need to shut out the noise of the world and *listen*. Other people's ideas of experiencing a situation do not have to be *our* definition. We each have the power to create our *own* life, with our own illusions and the power of our imagination and that is what we need to base our life on. We can all observe the same event and walk away with different perceptions of what we have seen. That is the beauty of illusion and imagination. Our goal is to change the perception of what we think is the reality, to see life through different glasses, and to reach out to heaven, listen to God, and begin to remember what we have forgotten.

The four questions most people ask about the power to create are:

- How do I achieve better health?
- How do I find my sole companion?
- How do I get my finances into better shape?
- How do I create a life without my loved one?

We are going to concentrate on health in this chapter. That is because prolonged grief usually takes its toll on people's health, and we find this goes hand in hand with the subject matter.

Health

Poor health is a huge issue in our society, a hell in the world today. Poor nutrition and the many abuses of the environment are an abomination to our body's immune system. As a species, we are not able to evolve quickly enough to fight off our external enemies. Also not to be forgotten are the types of weaponry, used in both today's warfare and that, of the twentieth century, which have destroyed the health of our troops and civilians around the world. Deserving of mention too are the good, old-fashioned diseases that we as humans inherit from one generation to the next. Today's Americans are grossly overweight and under-exercised, and diabetes is at an all-time high. With all this being said, we require "the power to create health" to fight off incurable diseases and to come out victorious. Is this possible? Yes, we believe it is. The major problem that we see here is the fact that we as Americans *don't listen.* To begin, we don't listen to what health care professionals say is "healthy" and "unhealthy." We eat fast food that is filled with calories and fat to clog up our digestive tracks and arteries. We don't even exercise enough to take a simple twenty-minute stroll down the block, checking in on neighbors or waving "hello." We instead are satisfied with picking up the remote and letting our fingers do the walking. Because we are such an undisciplined country, one of the hardest things for us to do is break a habit. Even if a physician tells us that we are going to die unless we quit smoking or eating a high-sodium diet, we can't do it. We can't break the habit to save our life until it brings us to the brink and almost takes our life. It takes lying in a hospital bed hooked up to tubes and monitors to hear the wake-up call. From that vantage point, some of us actually listen and make changes to our daily routine. However, most just bargain with God in the hospital room that they will change but, after recovery and time passes, foolishly think they have entered a safe zone and allow the habit to slowly return. How can we expect to conjure up what it takes to have the power to create health if we can't be diligent enough to do what is simple before things get complicated?

We forget that we have contracts here on Earth to fulfill not only with others, and ourselves but also with God and for the good of the world.

God has given us free will and therefore we have choices about what we put into our bodies, and how we shape and mold our health. But, in making those choices, we can't lose sight of our main objective which is of a spiritual nature: Are we taking care of what we have been given?

Yes, disease is a real wake-up call. When we come to a crossroads in our life, like facing cancer, we have to feel strong enough to take on the fight and come out on top. We realize that sounds like a lofty goal, but it is one that we believe *is* attainable. There is, however, one thing that must be clarified. Sometimes when we are diagnosed with an illness, it means that our journey here on Earth is over and it is time for us to return home. And, the act of going home means ending up on the side where we are now supposed to be.

Not all illnesses are curable. Even among patients with the same type of cancer, some are destined to survive and some are not. So, we must get ready for that day and for that battle. There are ways for us to start preparing right now, before a health crisis is upon us, to make sure we are ready to walk through that crisis with better understanding so we can make the right choices.

First of all, we need to learn how to pay attention to God, because he is speaking to us all the time. We hear him in the form of intuition or, as some call it, the Holy Spirit. We hear him in our heads when that little voice says "Get up and walk," "Don't eat that," "Sugar is not your friend." But, we simply filter God's voice out through our brains and rationalize how the next time we want to eat that sugar-filled yummy we will make a different choice or tomorrow we will go on that long-put-off walk. These are the early warning signs of pre-disease prevention. We need to listen carefully to each admonition in order to process what it is telling us. Only then can we agree with the message in the knowledge that it is for our highest good, and follow it up by acting on the guidance we are being given. We cannot emphasize enough how *important* this information is that we are being given. It is why we wrote this chapter for the book (and, undoubtedly, why you've taken your valuable time to read these words): to help you have a better understanding of the gifts that are being streamed down into us every day, all day, all the time. We must get out of our head and listen to our soul. How can we possibly think that we can help ourselves to create health or fight a life-threatening illness if we can't even do the small stuff?

Our soul has to know that we heed its messages so that, when we need it most, we can download what we have to do and act on it, no matter how difficult or how insane the instructions sound. If we learn to listen to ourselves about food—picking up an item to eat and hearing "No, this is not good for you" and making another choice—we will be able to make informed decisions about medical treatments. We will receive guidance about the right treatment for us, not only from our physician, but from the Higher Power through our soul. Yes, during a crisis, we will be sick, scared, and lost. Therefore, we must have this system in place so that we will be able to retrieve it during the most difficult times of our life. If a physician tells us a disease will take our life, we need to have the spiritual tools already in place to either say "no" and fight it or accept it with the knowledge that it's time to go home. Each of us will be the only one in charge of our own destiny, because we will be empowered by a relationship with God where he knows we are listening, as well as by the knowledge that we were sent here to serve God's children on his behalf and fulfill the contracts meant only for us. That is our shield and our sword! When we receive directions from our soul, we will have the discipline and stamina to follow through with what we must do. God will guide us.

If you are reading this and already are in the midst of fighting a health battle, it is not too late. You can begin right now to pray not only for yourself, but for others. You can create ideas about what you want to do for God's children, and then act on those ideas immediately even if it has to be in a very small form. In fact, if what you pray for yourself is only that you will be loving and of service to others, your soul will be cleansed a hundredfold. This is not a bargaining tool to use with God, but a humble approach to serving others. As long as you continue to serve others here on Earth for God, he will give you the guidance you seek. Pray for his counsel, and then listen to what he tells you. We can all do work for God's children and the environment in many ways that shower unconditional love on people and our world. We can pray for those who have no one to pray for them and for those who do not pray for themselves. Check in with your soul, listen to that little voice in your head, and take action on what it says. Remember, only you and your soul will know if it is time for you to go home or not.

Some of the biggest things we need to think about and remember are: What is my calling? Why am I here? What am I here to accomplish in this world to fulfill my goals with myself, for humanity, and for God? These questions can be answered by listening to our intuition, learning how to say yes, and then taking action. It is amazing how, if we are listening and acting on what our soul is telling us (no questions asked), one experience can lead to another. We will look around and not even fathom all the glorious wonder we have created around ourselves! But, we have to stay focused about what we are called to do and start using our remarkable gifts to help our planet and humanity. We are at a critical time now in our nation and in our world. We all have played a part in creating the destruction around us. Even more importantly, it is now up to us to create a new world filled with unconditional love and kindness. We have a long way to go in creating it. So, yes, create for your life and use these gifts every day, but don't lose sight of the true purpose behind the gifts. Create and channel grace for others and this new world.

Below, you will find a book list that includes three books with in-depth concepts about the power to create which you can read and listen to on your own. Then, you can put into practice some of the ideas that we already will have gone over in this chapter. The books are *The Emerald Tablet: Alchemy for Personal Transformation* by Dennis William Hauck (New York, Penquin Putnam, 1999), *Your Power to Create* by Caroline Myss (Audio CD, Learn Out Loud 2007), and Doreen Virtues *Divine Magic: The Seven Sacred Secrets of Manifestation* (Carlsbad, CA, HayHouse, 2006). These three resources will provide you with even more informative step-by-step approaches on how to take the power to create to further levels and dimensions in your life.

Our Concluding Words to You for Now . . .

We ask that you go back to the beginning of this book now and again answer the questions written on page 27. Please compare your thoughts and feelings from the earlier time with what you now believe and think. We hope you have been able to expand your knowledge and perhaps begin thinking about yourselves and your loved ones in a new and more spiritual way.

We thank you for taking the time and energy to read this book. We understand how difficult it is for grieving people to reach out and begin the healing process. But, by giving yourself that gift, you will have generated an opportunity to learn and most importantly connect with your loved one. You will understand that your loved one is not truly gone from your life. This doesn't mean that you won't continue to miss the smell of their hair, the touch of their face, the warmth of their hug, and their presence in your life in a physical way. However, your loved one *is* with you, and can see you in all your best and worst moments—not to judge you, but to continue to grant you their unconditional love!

As you have read in these pages, everything we experience impacts our soul's growth. Are you now able to see and understand the death of your loved one as a growth experience? Of course, you did not create or want this challenge and the resulting growth. It was presented to you and now, through this book, you are equipped with the tools to make this journey more meaningful and positive than it otherwise could have been.

Use your newfound tenacity to monitor your thoughts and reach out for your loving connections. Remember that thoughts create and, as such, you can continually build and strengthen those connections. Your task did not end when your loved one died. It was only the beginning, and we want to walk with you, side by side as you follow this healing pathway to a new normal and a new you.

The three of us send you our blessings as you venture forth and continue to work on your loving connections. We wish for you good energy, a strong connection with Spirit, and the wisdom to understand the process. Amen.

Meet the Girls

Jane   Sara   Deneene

JANE

Jane, who is from Kent, Ohio, is a counselor, teacher, writer and speaker. She enjoys working with people as they develop new spiritual, emotional, and mental perspectives on the thoughts and behaviors that create distress and dis-ease in their lives. Jane is a practicing counselor specializing in grief and clinical director of Counseling for Wellness, LLP. She has recently released her new book, *Loving Connections: The Healing Power of Afterdeath Communications* available on her website www.counselingforloss.com.

SARA

Sara Ruble, who is from Stow, Ohio, is the mother of Scott Michael Jessie. In 1994, Scott, who was Sara's only child, died suddenly of natural causes. He was only nineteen years old and the love of her life. Scott's death was a life-changing event for Sara. Being thrust into grief tested her daily. It has been a very difficult, but increasingly meaningful, journey. Sara's continuing relationship with Scott has brought her a renewed sense of peace, hope, and love.

DENEENE

Born in Chicago, Illinois, Deneene received her formal education at DePaul University, graduating with degrees in psychology, biology, and theology. For almost a decade, Deneene worked as a hospice spiritual care and bereavement counselor. She also had a private practice that included spiritual life coaching, grief counseling, and therapeutic touch. After working with hospice, she took out time for introspection and authored *The Angel Tales: Refuge for a Parent's Healing Heart.*

Spiritualityworkshops are proud to present their second and companion book to **Surviving and Thriving: Grief Relief & Continuing Relationships. Surviving and Thriving: Grief Relief & Continuing Relationships for the Professionals** contains all the information from the griever's book in addition to the information the professionals need to use these important and innovative techniques. This book is also available at www.spiritualityworkshops.com.

To reach us for any questions and upcoming workshops please visit our web site at www.spiritualityworkshops.com

Made in the USA